Pure Joy

Pure Joy

R. T. Kendall

Hodder & Stoughton
LONDON SYDNEY AUCKLAND

Unless otherwise noted, Scriptures are taken from the
HOLY BIBLE, NEW INTERNATIONAL VERSION.
Copyright © 1973, 1978, 1984 by International Bible Society.
Used by permission of Hodder & Stoughton. All rights reserved.
'NIV' is a registered trademark of International Bible Society.
UK trademark number 1448790.

Scriptures taken from *The Message* by Eugene H. Peterson,
copyright © 1993, 1994, 1995, 1996, 2000, 2001, 2002.
Used by permission of NavPress Publishing Group.
All rights reserved.

Scriptures noted AV are taken from the Authorised
(King James) Version of the Bible.

British Library Cataloguing in Publication Data
A record for this book is available from the British Library

ISBN 0 340 86194 0

Typeset in Bembo by Avon DataSet Ltd,
Bidford-on-Avon, Warwickshire

Printed and bound in Great Britain by
Bookmarque Ltd, Croydon, Surrey

The paper and board used in this paperback are natural
recyclable products made from wood grown in sustainable forests.
The manufacturing processes conform to the environmental
regulations of the country of origin.

Hodder & Stoughton
A Division of Hodder Headline Ltd
338 Euston Road
London NW1 3BH
www.madaboutbooks.com

To Dr David and Lil Onstad

Contents

Contents

Foreword

It is a delight to commend this book. A church minister who was all the rage in my youth was once warmly introduced to a clerical gathering as the man whose name was on all our lips, whose books were on all our shelves and whose illustrations were in all our sermons! I have to say that it's not just the illustrations here that might prove tempting to borrow but some of the chapter outlines also. They would go down well in the pulpit. But this book is not just for pulpit people, it's clearly for pew folk as well.

R.T. has a gift for making the complicated simple, for showing that subjects that could seem commonplace are really important to talk about, and that questions thought too dumb to mention are often too vital to overlook. He has a knack for making the ordinary both interesting and edifying.

The book contains a series of reflections and expositions of a number of relevant biblical texts. It is illustrated with relevant stories from the lives of others and practical personal experiences from his own. This is all expressed with refreshing common sense and spelt out against the background of his orthodox theology – all very readable and digestible.

The subject of joy, which is such an important and lovely gift of the Holy Spirit, has too often been glossed over. We have not known of such a happy treatment of 'true joy' since Professor C.S. Lewis described his personal experiences in his *Surprised by Joy*. Or Canon Guy King, a popular Keswick speaker, published his delightful little commentary on St Paul's letter to the Philippians, and invited his readers to walk the *Joy Way* through it with him. R. T. deals with both the sudden experiences of joy and the life long expressions of it – the crisis of taking it in and the process of working it out.

Quite clearly Jesus was *anointed* with joy but he was equally *acquainted* with grief, and R. T. does not gloss over this seeming paradox of Christian experience. I liked the comment of his ageing mother when she said that she had been tried and tested so often by that stage in life that she found it difficult to know the difference between the joy and the pain. She had discovered something very fundamental. Those who get to read this book may well be on the road to making the same discovery and growing into the same maturity.

I have been very refreshed through reading *Pure Joy* and I sincerely hope that many others will be too. My prayer is that they will.

David Pytches
Chorleywood
October 2003

Preface

About five months ago I was standing and singing in a service in which I was shortly to be introduced to preach. For some reason – instead of worshipping as I had been doing – I suddenly, but strangely, found myself thinking, 'I bet that David Moloney of Hodder will be writing to me soon to ask what book I would like to write next, and I wonder what I will tell him?' Two seconds later the words 'pure joy' just came to me and instantly I began to envisage chapter headings. I sat down at once in the front pew, took out a pen, and wrote on a slip of paper certain headings that came into my head as quickly as I could jot them down. The next thing I knew I was being introduced to speak, but those headings that came to me that day are the chapters in this book.

When I arrived home in Key Largo three days later, there was an e-mail from David Moloney. He said he was writing because he thought it was time to talk about another book and did I have anything in mind? Yes! I wrote to him at once, telling him what I have just written above. He replied affirming my title and subject matter and, in what seemed like no time at all, another book was on the way.

Not all my books come that way, and I certainly don't recall another one of them having a beginning like that! Also, this is not to claim that it means you must regard this book as being totally divinely inspired, although I think that it certainly is in measure – much like I feel when I am preparing a sermon or preaching. Only the Bible is the infallible, inspired word of God and is to be read and believed wholeheartedly. Therefore a book or a sermon has but limited inspiration and is to be read critically. But to the degree that what follows is biblically and theologically sound – and truly written in the Spirit – I pray that will be the degree to which God will use this book powerfully in your life.

This is not a book of sermons, and I typed every word myself! But I have still needed help and input from my former secretary at Westminster Chapel, Beryl Grogan (with the gracious permission of her new boss, and my wonderful successor, Greg Haslam), in tidying up the manuscript. I have spent the better part of the last five months writing these lines – in between speaking engagements – when my wife Louise and I are not travelling. Louise has been at my side as I have typed, and has helped me again and again as I have worked on this book. I thank Linda Crosby for the careful editing she has done. I thank also the staff of Hodder & Stoughton for their hard work in preparing this book for publication, and especially David Moloney for his usual wisdom and encouragement.

This book is lovingly dedicated to Dr and Mrs David Onstad, our precious friends in Fort Lauderdale, Florida. May God bless you all.

R. T. Kendall
January 2003
Key Largo, Florida
www.rtkendallministries.com

Introduction

Some of my friends may laugh out loud when they see that I have written a book called *Pure Joy*. One friend entered into a covenant with me that if he prayed every day for God to put a smile on my face, I would in turn pray daily along a certain line for him. We have now been doing this for each other for many years. His prayer for me has not been answered, so how dare I write a book on 'joy'!

The answer I believe is this. Joy is a fruit of the Holy Spirit (Gal. 5:22), but a smile on one's face may have more to do with one's natural temperament and personality. I know people who have a smile on their faces all the time, but it is hardly the joy of the Lord, for these people I am talking about aren't even Christians! I know one Christian lady who always seems to have a smile on her face. One day I asked her about this beautiful smile and she graciously admitted that it actually camouflaged a very sad heart, and

1

that she was not the cheerful, happy person her smile suggested.

A Christian who has a radiant smile – whether in church or out shopping – is indeed a wonderful witness to the Christian faith. There is little doubt about that. And those of us who by nature look sad or depressed all the time are not good testimonies. That's me. I seldom smile. I'm a photographer's nightmare. Any picture you see of me smiling is the result of the hard work of people saying 'cheese', and standing on their heads or something like that!

But I learned something when some of us in Westminster Chapel began the Pilot Light ministry (witnessing in the streets of Victoria) in 1982. If I smiled, people were more likely to take a tract, but if I looked nervous (which I was at first) or gloomy (which is all too characteristic of me much of the time!), these people didn't want my literature. So I forced a smile and it worked. I managed to look pleasant, even if I did not feel like it, and I had far greater results.

When I phoned Louise from Israel in July 2002 to pray for me, because the next day I would be meeting with Yasser Arafat, she urged me to smile! My friends Alan Bell and Lyndon Bowring went into the Ramallah compound and prayed hard, but quietly, for me when I witnessed to Arafat – that I would smile. And the power of their prayers, and the smile itself, worked there as well.

So I need to say right at the start of this book that the joy referred to here is not necessarily reflected in a person's smile, neither is it what people today commonly call 'happiness'. Happiness, a state that one enjoys because of good things that 'happen' to fall one's way, is largely produced by external things: a good job, a house, material things, friends or financial security. The cause of such happiness is outward.

But joy is inward. Our Lord Jesus was a man of sorrows (Isa. 53:3), but he could speak of his joy (John 15:11, 17:13). I doubt he had a great smile on his face when he was on the cross crying out, 'My God, my God, why have you forsaken me?' (Matt. 27:46), but he endured it all because of the joy that was set before him (Heb. 12:2). We therefore are not required to look cheerful or buoyant when in a deep trial, but we can still have pure joy the whole time simply because we know what is waiting for us down the road if we don't give up.

There has been a rediscovery in recent years of the so-called 'four temperaments' that Hippocrates (600 BC) claimed applied to all people in some way. He thought that mankind could be divided into one of four basic temperaments – the phlegmatic, the sanguine, the melancholy and the choleric – and that every person had one of these as their dominant trait. The phlegmatic person is generally laid-back, softly spoken, easy-going, not easily ruffled, and almost always much the same. The sanguine individual is cheerful, the life and soul of the party, talkative, and usually popular. The melancholy is often the thinker – Hippocrates said all philosophers are melancholy – but also prone to being sad and depressive. The choleric is domineering, one who always takes control, is pushy, and may have leadership potential. In our Pilot Light course at Westminster Chapel, we referred to these temperaments to show that God can use more than one 'type' to be an effective soul-winner on the streets.

Obviously you can press these distinctions too far, but my point is this: one's temperament is irrelevant when it comes to real joy. Those who *appear* to have it may not have it, and those who seem the opposite may in fact possess pure joy. I say this to encourage any reader who may have felt guilty – like myself – for not appearing to be joyful, or who does not always feel joyful, but who may none the less have pure joy.

And yet there are those whose countenances have been shaped by the joy of the Lord, and it has become in some ways a part of their personality and identity. I have known people like this. Harold Wiles, a former deacon of Westminster Chapel (now in heaven), was such a blessing to have in the congregation because his pleasant appearance and shine on his countenance became an inspiration to preach to. Dr Martyn Lloyd-Jones used to talk about a man he noticed in a certain congregation when he annually preached in Wales. Every year, this man took the same seat in the balcony. His face shone in such a manner that Dr Lloyd-Jones told me that if he was ever in difficulty as he preached (which alone encouraged me!), he would simply look at this man and immediately start preaching better! One day Dr Lloyd-Jones enquired about the man, who turned out to be a retired Pentecostal preacher. When I was a boy I was deeply impacted by a book written by Dr Harry Jessup called *I Met a Man with a Smiling Face*. The author traced the man's countenance to the baptism of the Holy Spirit.

Moses must have had this at times. When he came down from Mount Sinai he was 'not aware that his face was radiant because he had spoken with the LORD' (Exod. 34:29). This had nothing do with temperament, but his joy must have been tremendous. When Stephen testified before the Sanhedrin, those who witnessed the occasion 'saw that his face was like the face of an angel' (Acts 6:15). He had a joy that made him utterly fearless before hostile men.

This book is not a justification for those of us who look sad, but may in fact have some joy. Although we don't need to be silly people who pretend they are happy all the time, because our testimony is important, we should not cave in to the way we sometimes feel. It could not have blessed the people at Westminster Chapel in my early days when I appeared melancholy and sober because of the small congregations. Fear showed all over my face when I took the chair and bowed my head to look pious. I later determined to make myself look pleasant, and I could feel that the people were then more inclined to enjoy the worship and the preaching. They needed to know I was OK! But more than that, it pleased the Lord that I was not going to be influenced by how many were out there to preach to, but by his promise to be faithful. I got my joy from knowing that he was with me, knew how I felt, had given me a definite word for the people, and that what I said would change lives. And guess what! I began to feel the joy of the Lord more than ever. And it showed.

The first promise of the gospel was announced by the angels to the shepherds: 'I bring you good news of great joy that will be for all people' (Luke 2:10). When the Magi saw the star that they had temporarily lost sight of, they were 'overjoyed' (AV: 'rejoiced with exceeding great joy' –

Matt. 2:10). The Christian faith and message promise joy – pure joy. Not what people call happiness, but joy. Not health or wealth, but joy. Not an easy ride and fun, but joy. We are filled with 'an inexpressible and glorious joy' (AV: 'joy unspeakable and full of glory' – 1 Pet. 1:8).

The word 'joy' (Greek *chara*) appears fifty-nine times in the New Testament. The seventy that Jesus sent out into the villages 'returned with joy' because of the new authority they had been given (Luke 10:17). Great joy came in the city of Samaria because of signs, wonders and miracles (Acts 8:6–8). There is joy in heaven over one sinner who repents (Luke 15:7). Despite being persecuted and rejected, the disciples 'were filled with joy and with the Holy Spirit' (Acts 13:52). The conversion of the Gentiles made Jewish believers 'very glad' (AV: 'great joy' – Acts 15:3). The kingdom of God is righteousness, peace and 'joy in the Holy Spirit' (Rom. 14:17).

The word 'rejoicing' is used seventy-four times. If we are insulted and falsely accused because of Jesus, we are told to 'rejoice and be glad' because of our reward in heaven (Matt. 5:12). We should rejoice not because of authority over demons (which obviously produces joy), but because our 'names are written in heaven' (Luke 10:20). Love rejoices with the truth (1 Cor. 13:6). We are commanded to rejoice in the Lord always (Phil. 3:1; 4:4) and to rejoice for the privilege of participating in the sufferings of Christ (1 Pet. 4:13).

However, the distinction I have made between joy and happiness is not so acute in the New Testament. The Greek word *makarios* (used fifty-eight times) is sometimes translated as 'blessed', but sometimes 'happy' (1 Pet. 4:14, AV). In fact, the Authorised Version prefers the word 'happy' at least six times (e.g. Acts 26:2, John 13:17, Rom. 14:22). Its use in the Beatitudes (Matt. 5:3–12) could most aptly be translated as 'congratulations'. But the 'happiness' used in New Testament Greek is not so much from outward circumstances, but tends instead to mean the same as inward joy.

The way we use the word 'happiness' today is rather different. Its etymology can be traced to a word that nowadays would probably mean 'luck'. In the parable of the Good Samaritan, Jesus described the priest who 'happened' to be going down the same road (AV: 'by chance' – Luke 10:31). This later came to be called 'happiness' because of what 'happens' due to chance. Therefore the word today would mean what people call luck, or simply that you are happy because you have been lucky. Such 'happiness' is therefore a long way from the joy or blessedness inherent in the gospel of Jesus Christ.

Thomas Jefferson, one of the founding fathers of the American Constitution, wrote that all people have the right to the 'pursuit of happiness'. But Christians have the right to the pursuit of *joy* instead, and are indeed promised it by virtue of the very gospel of Christ. It begins with the joy of forgiveness of sins and ends with the promise of heaven, which will never end. It is there that we receive the ultimate bliss – but along the way we are given a promise of . . . pure joy.

Dignifying the Trial

Consider it pure joy, my brothers, whenever you face trials of many kinds, because you know that the testing of your faith develops perseverance. (James 1:2–3)

It is not every day that I can remember where I was when 'the penny dropped' with regard to understanding a particular verse in the Bible, but I do when it comes to James 1:2. It came not at the end of a forty-day fast or an all-night prayer meeting. It was when I came to myself after losing my temper in a pizza shop in Kissimmee, Florida, in the summer of 1979. I had *so* looked forward to a pizza in this particular place and regarded such as a measure of compensation for having to return to Disney World a second year in a row. But when the time came, everything went wrong: as a result of driving rain, my pizzas fell out of a wet paper bag into a puddle of water, and now

I had to face the same manager of the pizza shop – to which I returned – after telling him off for taking forty-five minutes in the first place. 'How could all this happen?' I asked myself.

But James 1:2 had already been on my mind for weeks since I had planned to start preaching on the little book of James at Westminster Chapel in the autumn. As I drove back to the pizza shop that evening, I said to myself, 'Either James 1:2 is true or it isn't, and if I plan to preach on it shortly I had better begin practising what I preach.'

This trial of having everything go wrong regarding a long-awaited pizza at a time when people are starving, hurting, living in poverty or financial insecurity – or are ill with pain – is almost too silly to mention. It was hardly the greatest trial one could suffer. But I have to tell you, this episode was pivotal for me, and I came to my senses for being so upset. At the same time, it was a trial for me – although perhaps I should call it 'testing' instead. In any case, minutes before I returned to the pizza shop to apologise with genuine meekness to the manager, I repented before God for my anger and behaviour. In that moment I decided to 'dignify' this trial, and that is when a new phrase was born to me – 'dignifying the trial'.

Jesus taught us that they who are faithful in that which is least – or in little things – are the ones who will be faithful in much – bigger things (Luke 16:10). That is why that pizza story is so important to me. I decided then and there to *dignify* that situation by accepting the entire matter as something God sent. It was a divine set-up. I not only repented to the Lord, but thanked him for the whole thing.

I apologised to the manager and cheerfully waited for another pizza (for some reason, he wouldn't let me pay) and returned to my family at the motel a different person.

As I put it in my book *In Pursuit of His Glory*, that little testing in Kissimmee was to prepare me for far, far greater trials that came all too swiftly after that. But had I not 'passed' that test; it would require God to send yet another equivalent trial down the road before I could be trusted with greater difficulties. What makes me blush most is the thought that God had been sending such trials over the years, but I never saw them as blessings, or opportunities. I just battled through them somehow and got over the difficulty as soon as I could, but I was not one whit better for it as a result. Fortunately, God got my attention in Kissimmee, probably (I am ashamed to add) because I would be forced to preach on it.

However, to preach on challenging texts over the years has been the way, it seems to me, that God has put a pistol to my head to sort me out. My anointing to preach has always been linked to the Holy Spirit's direct help – sermon by sermon. Some ministers are probably so gifted that they do not need the Spirit's help in the way that I have done. They could flow because of their natural ability, intellect, knowledge of the Bible and commentaries. But I was made, it seems to me, in such a manner that I was not allowed to do that. I have envied fellow ministers with such great learning or oratorical eloquence that it allowed them to preach with ease and without apparently having to plead with God on their knees. It just came to them naturally. God has not done that with me. I have had to have the Holy

Spirit's immediate anointing or I was helpless. This is not a statement of humility; it is just a fact. I have said this simply to point out that I could not have preached on James 1:2 with the blessing of God had I myself not been forced to dignify that trial. And yet by doing so in my personal life God came through by giving me more insights, as well as an ability to communicate.

Counting it *pure joy* to face the fact of my natural lack of brilliance is what I have had to do for many years. I know also that people often laugh or roll their eyes heavenwards when they hear me talk like this, as many think I am far more gifted than I really am. They don't know that it is the Holy Spirit who has managed to break through to me *because* I need unusual help, and that I have received such help *because* God managed to make me more teachable. God chose not to give me the brain of a John Calvin or a Jonathan Edwards; neither did he give me the oratory of a Charles Spurgeon or a Martyn Lloyd-Jones. And yet he chose to give me a respectable platform from which to preach! What was I to do? I chose to count my insufficiency for these things *pure joy* in order that God would use me – not to mention get the glory.

What the Authorised Version translates as 'count' it all joy, the New International Version translates as 'consider' it pure joy. The Greek word is *heegeomai*; it means to value highly, to esteem. Paul used this when he said to King Agrippa, 'I consider myself fortunate to stand before you today' (Acts 26:2). Moses 'regarded' disgrace for the sake of Christ as of greater value than the treasures of Egypt because he was looking ahead to his reward (Heb. 11:26).

We therefore are to consider having to face trials of many kinds as pure joy. It is thus a word often used in an ironic sense. What would naturally make us feel the opposite – to be upset or feel sorry for ourselves – is to be taken as a wonderful privilege, or opportunity, instead.

Who enjoys the feeling of disgrace? It would, after all, be abnormal to enjoy this. Unless, that is, one had a definite reason for feeling this way. Moses did. He considered disgrace as more valuable than earthly luxury – all because it put him in good stead for the future. Jesus endured the cross because of the joy set before him (Heb. 12:2). The apostle Paul used *heegeomai* when he referred to the 'pluses' of his background – being circumcised the eighth day, being of the stock of Israel and of the tribe of Benjamin, being a Pharisee, and faultless as to legalistic righteousness. He *considered* these things not pluses, but minuses – all because of the dazzling privilege of knowing Jesus. That is simply the way he regarded those things that most people would love (Phil. 3:5–8).

This is what James wants us to do when we face trials of many kinds: consider them pure joy. It doesn't make sense! And yet it does! He tells us to consider trials as pure joy because of what they do for us *if* we believe and apply these words. It will be seen to make very good sense indeed. James wants us to see it now – by faith. Moses did what he did – regarding disgrace for the sake of Jesus of inestimable value – by faith; and he was never sorry he made that choice. Neither will any of us be.

And yet it is not easy to do this. James puts a task before us that is exceedingly difficult. It compares with what Josif

Tson once said to me, 'R.T., you must totally forgive them,' when I was in a time of near despair. I said to him, 'I can't.' He replied, 'You can and you must.' It wasn't easy, but it was the greatest thing I ever did. So too with dignifying a trial. It is not easy.

How, then, are we to begin to regard trials as pure joy? Only by sufficient motivation. We must be inspired or stimulated to look at trials in a positive manner. In Moses' case it was because of the reward he believed would be his later on. He was absolutely right. It was even what motivated Jesus. Imagine that! It was the joy that lay ahead that kept him going. He was not enjoying the cross. Not for a second. He did not relish the physical pain. He did not enjoy all the taunts of 'He saved others, but he can't save himself' (Mark 15:31). It must have added to his suffering to see Mary Magdalene sobbing her heart out at the foot of the cross – when he could not give her a single word of comfort. How did he manage? He knew it would be worth it all if he stuck it out without murmuring. It was because of the great joy that was going to be his that he was able to endure the cross. He considered it pure joy because pure joy was coming. And it came!

James tells us therefore that trials are a good thing – if we have a positive attitude towards them when they come. He certainly doesn't say we will enjoy them. Instead, we endure them. But we regard the thought of them as pure joy because of what these trials can do for us. They are, says Peter, more precious than gold (1 Pet. 1:7).

Imagine a congregation of 100 people. Suppose we could hear each person's story of hardship. Some of those stories might relate to a deep hurt – of a misdeed or injustice done to them; some might have lost a fortune; some have been lied about; some have suffered physically, or mentally; some cry out for vindication. Let us say we all vote on the 'top ten' – those who in our estimation suffered the most out of the 100 people present. Let us then say we narrow the list down to three. Finally, we pick the person we believe has suffered the most out of the 100 present. Now imagine that you were in that congregation and not only got short-listed, but were voted to be the person in the congregation who, by all accounts, had suffered more than anyone else in that room.

How would you feel? What do you suppose you would say? Perhaps you would say, 'See, I told you I had suffered more than anybody else.' And suppose we all agreed, that you have suffered more than anybody we have ever met? What would you expect then? Would you want us to gather around you and say, 'We are very sorry for you. We had no idea how much you have suffered. I don't know how you managed'? Is that what you would want? Would you feel somewhat compensated so you could say to us, 'I told you how much I have suffered'? What would this do for you? Would you be any better off? You may say, 'At least I would feel better, that all those people around me realised how much I have suffered.' I can appreciate that. But are you *really* better off? The truth is, it does feel good when others are sympathetic – but only to a degree. Suppose someone says 'Congratulations!' But the danger is that we could become insatiable in wanting people to know what we have gone through. If all we want is for *people* to know, *that* is all the 'reward' we will get. But if we get our joy from knowing *God* knows, we qualify for the honour that only he can bring (John 5:44).

My mother grew up in Springfield, Illinois. She was influenced by a very old woman who lived to be ninety. This woman once said to my mother, 'I have served the Lord for so long now that I can hardly tell the difference between a blessing and a trial.' This lady had learned the very lesson that James puts before us; and the reason I am writing this chapter is for all of us to learn this lesson.

The greater the suffering, the greater the anointing. If it is anointing you want, then expect suffering. If it is a great anointing you want, anticipate great suffering at some stage. The anointing is the power of the Holy Spirit to make us do what we do with ease and without fatigue. The main reason for burn-out and fatigue is almost certainly because someone has gone beyond their anointing; they went outside it rather than functioning within it. It was because they could not accept the limits of their ability. None of us can do everything, but to the person who is not content with the anointing or gift that he or she has, there will be trouble ahead. It is humbling to accept our limits, but there is considerable joy and peace in doing so, not to mention an increase of anointing. We can pray for a greater anointing – namely, an ability to do what we previously could not do in our own strength – but until that anointing has come, we must accept the limits of our faith and our ability.

I myself would prefer a greater anointing than anything. It is literally what I want most in the entire world. In a word: more of God. This way, I can achieve all he wants of me. He never promotes us to the level of our incompetence. As long as we are content with the calling he has chosen for us, we will live and move at the level he has seen fit to give us. This is partly what is meant when the psalmist said, 'He chose our inheritance for us' (Ps. 47:4). It can be a testing in itself when we come to terms with his determination of what talent he has decided to give us. We may envy another's anointing. It is the way Peter felt when told how he would die, and all he could apparently think of is how John would die. Jesus replied, in so many words, 'That's none of your business – just follow me and quit looking over your shoulder' (see John 21:18–23).

A.W. Tozer used to say that we could have as much of God as we want. When I first came across this comment I disagreed. But I know now what he meant. We do not prove how much we want of God merely by the intense desire at the moment. We prove it by how we react to circumstances in life, and the opportunities given to us to do such things dignify the trials he hands to us on our silver platter.

When we are content with the anointing God chose for us, we do what we are called to do without fatigue. 'I can do everything through him who gives me strength' (Phil. 4:13). When I become mentally and emotionally fatigued in what I am doing, it is a fairly strong hint that I have chosen to move outside my anointing and what God specifically asked me to do. As long as I do *what* he called me to do and *no more*, I will not be edging towards burn-out.

And yet I would like to have more anointing than I have! This is a legitimate desire because Paul told us to desire earnestly the greater gifts (1 Cor. 12:31). God will answer this request so long as it is sought with his glory in mind; he will answer the request if it is his will (1 John 5:14). God will consequently supply the need for this by granting the necessary anointing required for what I am called to do.

If, then, it is a greater anointing I truly want, and I wake up with one big enormous trial before me, I should grasp it with both hands! I must consider this trial pure joy! This is because the trial is a fairly strong hint from the Lord Jesus that I am going to receive the anointing I long for. He knows what I want more than anything, so if he sends a trial or testing my way, then I have every reason to believe that the anointing I long for is coming – if I dignify the trial at hand.

James does not specifically use the word 'anointing' when he tries to motivate his readers to consider their trials as pure joy. He uses the equivalent, however, and it comes to the exact same thing. His words are: 'because you know that the testing of your faith develops perseverance' (Jas. 1:3). You may be disappointed at first that only perseverance seems to be the immediate goal of dignifying the trial. 'I wanted more than that out of all I've been going through', you may honestly say or feel. I understand this.

But perseverance is the gateway to what is right and achievable. It is the next step forward – the link to a brilliant future. God does not lead us from A to Z, but from A to B. During the trial, the immediate need is perseverance, or patience. The Greek word is *hupomonee*. It is used thirty-two times in the New Testament and is usually translated as 'patience' in the Authorised Version. It is a word that partly means bravery, but also the ability to endure under imposed sufferings and temptation.

And yet this perseverance is not the main goal. It is not the ultimate goal. But it *is* what enables you to reach the goal that James envisages: 'Perseverance must finish its work so that you may be mature and complete, not lacking anything' (James 1:4). This means a peace and contentment so vast and so profound that you no longer crave what you once thought was so important to you. 'The LORD is my Shepherd, I shall not want' (Ps. 23:1, AV). James sees a time ahead for the person who dignifies the trial that will mean indescribable peace, the highest level of anointing, the soul uncluttered by greed, and a heart filled with the very presence of God. It is pure joy.

In other words, if you consider a trial to be pure joy, it will lead to pure joy. Count it pure joy, call it pure joy, regard the trial as pure joy, and one day you will experience pure joy for yourself. I promise it!

This is why I had to deal with James 1:2 in the first chapter of this book. All that follows will, sooner or later, pass through the fiery trial God ordains for us. God *can* of course give pure joy directly and immediately by the Holy Spirit's coming on us – without any need to dignify the trial. Sometimes he does! But his normal, predictable, promised and guaranteed way of leading us to pure joy is by bringing us to *reckon* the trial as pure joy. Impute the trial with pure joy. This is the word Paul uses for justification by faith: faith 'counts' or is 'credited' as righteousness (Rom. 4:3). We should do this regarding trials: see pure joy in the trial, just as God sees righteousness in us when we believe.

Regarding the trial itself as 'pure joy', then, is what I mean by dignifying that trial. To dignify means to bestow honour upon. When I dignify a trial I treat it with honour and respect. Indeed, a trial is my 'glory'. That is exactly what Paul said, 'I ask you, therefore, not to be discouraged because of my sufferings for you, which are your glory' (Eph. 3:13). We should actually treat a trial with the same respect as we would Her Majesty the Queen or a head of state. After all, the trials God ordains for us come from His Majesty King Jesus:

> Every joy or trial falleth from above,
> Traced upon our dial by the Sun of Love
> We may trust him fully, all for us to do;
> They who trust Him wholly find Him wholly true.
>
> *Frances Ridley Havergal (1836–79)*

Trials are predestined. Paul urged that we be not 'unsettled' by these trials; for you know 'quite well that we were destined for them' (1 Thess. 3:3). Consider this, 'it has been granted to you on behalf of Christ not only to believe on him, but also to suffer for him' (Phil. 1:29). The suffering that God ordains need not be persecution only, for if trials sent from God were only persecution, some people would not suffer much at all. Any trial that God sends – death of a loved one or friend, financial reverse, loss, illness, misunderstanding, losing your keys, failure, disappointment, betrayal, abuse, unemployment, losing a job, mental or emotional depression, accident, loneliness, missing a train or plane, rejection, not getting that important invitation, toothache, a headache or any physical pain – should be seen as having our Lord's handprints all over them.

There is a difference between trial and temptation, although both come from the same Greek word – *peirasmos*. They are often used interchangeably, though. After all, temptation is a trial (of faith) and every trial is a temptation (to grumble). When the word appears in the New Testament the context helps us to see which meaning is meant. There are therefore differences and similarities between trials and temptations. Although we must not push the distinctions too far, here are examples of the differences:

1 *In their ultimate origin*. Temptations come from the flesh; trials are sent from God. 'When tempted, no-one should say, "God is tempting me." For God cannot be tempted by evil, nor does he tempt anyone' (Jas. 1:13). God 'tested' Abraham (Gen. 22:1); God allows temptation. He allowed Satan to test Job (Job 1:6–12). Therefore when we speak of 'trial' we see God's fingerprints; when we see temptation, we see our own – or the devil's.

2 *In their immediate origin*. Temptation comes from within; trials usually come from outside us. '. . . each one is tempted when, by his own evil desire, he is dragged away and enticed' (Jas. 1:14). Trials are allowed from God, as when Satan was given permission to go so far – but no further – with Job. Job suffered physically, but inwardly – at least at first – there was no apparent struggle.

3   In *their moral relevance*. Temptation, when it is sexual in nature, has considerable moral relevance, but a trial may be what I would want to call morally neutral, such as illness or losing one's keys.

4   *With reference to what is tested*. Temptation will usually attack a weak spot; trials test our strength as well as exposing a weakness we may have been unaware of – as with Job, who turned out to be so self-righteous.

What are the similarities between trial and temptation?

1   *Both are by God's sovereign permission*. Whether it is labelled trial or temptation, you can be absolutely sure that God allowed it.

2   *The devil will try to exploit either*. You can be sure that Satan will take every possible advantage of us. If it is temptation, he will do everything he can to get us to succumb. If it is a trial, he will try to get us to grumble or to accuse God for unfairness in allowing it.

3   *The timing is always 'bad'*. In other words, they never come at a 'good' time, when we feel 'now would be a good time for the devil to have a go' (as if that were a wise comment – which it isn't). Satan loves to take us by surprise and, even when we imagine ourselves strong, the devil is clever enough to exploit a weak spot that we had not been aware of. In any case, keep 1 Corinthians 10:12 in mind: 'So, if you think you are standing firm, be careful that you don't fall!'

4   *Both are within our ability to cope*. This may be called 'God's filtering grace'. Every trial or temptation passes through

God's faithful filter. God's filtering process – by which he determines what passes from his hand to where we are – is tailor-made for every one of us. 'No temptation [or trial – remember that it comes from the same Greek word] has seized you except what is common to man. And God is faithful; he will not let you be tempted [or tried] beyond what you can bear. But when you are tempted, he will also provide a way out so that you can stand up under it' (1 Cor. 10:13). This is one of the greatest verses in Holy Scripture. It also proves that God allows temptation and implies that he could have stopped it had he chosen to do so. I therefore conclude that all trials or temptations that come our way have already passed through the Throne of Grace and God 'OK-ed' it before it reached us. It passed through his filter.

5   *Both are accompanied by the devil's suggestion – 'give in'.* The devil will invariably come alongside and say, 'Give in, give up, cave in to the temptation, cave in to this trial – it is too much for you.' As for temptation, the devil will also make it seem 'providential' – that is, he will make it appear to be in God's will at the moment for you to succumb since it was timed in such a manner that God himself willed you to give in on this particular occasion. That is the way the devil's evil mind works. I think of Paul's comment regarding Satan, 'we are not unaware of his schemes' (2 Cor. 2:11). It works this way whether it is a trial or a temptation; the devil will always try to make you think that it is beyond your ability to cope.

Every trial sent from God has a built-in time limit, and the trial you are in won't last for ever! It may seem as though it will never end, but it will. *It will end*. And once it is over, we must ask ourselves a hard question: did we pass or fail the test? To dignify the trial is to pass the test; to treat the trial with contempt – to dishonour it – is to fail the test. The trial might even end suddenly – this is not uncommon – and find us blushing because we were murmuring and complaining right to the end. Believe me, I know what it is *not* to dignify a trial. I am sorry to say that I lived that way for years. When it was over, it was over; I myself was no better off, only that I mopped my brow and said, like the predestinarian who fell down the stairs, 'I'm sure glad that's over.' It is not a good feeling to realise, once it is over, that you did not dignify the trial, but it is a good, good feeling indeed to know, when it has ended, that you did dignify it.

So how do we dignify a trial?

1. *Welcome it.* Welcome the trial as you would welcome the Holy Spirit, for it is the Holy Spirit, the Third Person of the Godhead, who is with the Father and the Son, behind the whole ordeal. I love Chris Bowater's song, 'Holy Spirit, we welcome you'. I do not say you will be as intense in your welcome, for it is not a pleasant moment. But welcome the trial anyway and say to the Lord, 'I know you have sent this to me and I want to get the maximum benefit you have in mind when you ordained it.' This is to begin to dignify the trial from the first moment. No, you will not be thrilled to your fingertips. The beginning of the trial can be painful, like

an unwelcome guest who unexpectedly knocks on your door. You will treat that guest with respect, especially if it is a person you admire; and if you can be courteous and polite to an unwelcome guest, then surely you would want to be that way with the King of kings when he comes knocking at your door to test you! And in this case, he comes with one purpose: for your own good.

2 *Don't panic.* Satan's immediate goal when he is given permission to attack is to get you to panic. This is why he is compared to a lion – a roaring lion (1 Pet. 5:8). The reason for the roar is to intimidate and cause fear and panic – to make you think you are defeated even before anything has had a chance to happen. In the jungle a lion roars to scare his prey and make the little animal feel defeated before the lion has even attacked. The devil is like that. When your enemy comes in like a violent storm, don't panic! Remember: God 'OK-ed' it before it came to you. He reckoned you were able to cope or he would not have allowed it. God never operates outside the verse we looked at above, 1 Corinthians 10:13. Realise this as soon as you can – say to yourself, 'God allowed this for a purpose. He would not have allowed this if there were no way of coping.' As the psalmist put it, '. . . do not fret – it leads only to evil' (Ps. 37:8).

3 *See the trial as a compliment to you from God himself.* This is important. The kind of trial he has allowed you to have is very possibly one that could not be granted to others around you. Whereas your first reaction

(understandably) is to feel sorry for yourself, on reflection you should be able to see that God gave this trial to you for one reason: you are up to it. You should hear the word 'congratulations' when the trial has come your way. The best translation of the word *makarios* (usually translated 'blessed' in the Beatitudes) is 'congratulations'. Substitute the word 'congratulations' when you come to 'Beatitude' and you will get the purest meaning of the word. For example, 'Congratulations are the poor in spirit, for theirs is the kingdom of heaven. Congratulations are those who mourn . . .' etc. For Jesus is saying that this means that the person who experiences those things described in Matthew 5:3–12 is regarded as special. The future is bright – very bright indeed – for that person who is poor in spirit, who mourns, who is meek, who hungers and thirsts for righteousness, etc. But, like it or not, the process begins with being poor in spirit because this is normally the way that God gets our attention.

4   *Never forget that God allowed it.* This point must be stressed again and again because Satan will want us to focus within and feel sorry for ourselves, and then start to point the finger at someone rather than to stop and realise: this scenario has passed through God's filtering process. He allowed it. He could have stopped it, yes, but he didn't. 'Why, Lord? Why me, Lord?' is the most natural question to emerge. Even Jesus asked God 'Why?' when he was suffering the worst (Matt. 27:46). So it is not sinful to ask 'Why?' It is sinful only when you become bitter and shake your fist in God's face. Don't

ever do that. It will get you nowhere. This is partly what is meant by James's words later: 'the wrath of man worketh not the righteousness of God' (Jas. 1:20, AV). Becoming bitter and angry with God will not coax him to feel sorry for you; it will only delay your experiencing what God wants for you. Moreover, being bitter is the very opposite to dignifying the trial. Try not to get hung up on the vexing theological issue of whether God caused – or only permitted – this or that to happen. There is a fine line between the two and nobody in the history of the world has solved this one. So whether it be physical pain or losing your keys, it does not matter whether God caused it or simply let it happen. You know this much: he did let it happen. Let your case rest there. Our task is to dignify that trial, whether it is big or small.

5 *Know that there is a purpose in it*. This is vital. Were it not for this, there would be no point in counting trials 'pure joy'. The reason you can safely do so is because there is an intelligent, meaningful *reason* God allowed it. James actually gives the immediate reason: to develop perseverance that leads to pure joy that is so wonderful that we lack nothing. Here is the way our passage in James is translated by Eugene H. Peterson in *The Message*: 'Consider it a sheer gift, friends, when tests and challenges come at you from all sides. You know that under pressure, your faith-life is forced into the open and shows its true colours. So don't try to get out of anything prematurely. Let it do its work so you become mature and well-developed, not deficient in any way.'

This further demonstrates that there is purpose in the trial that God brings to our lives. It is to refine us. To teach us a lesson. To make us better equipped. To make us more sensitive. To teach us self-control. To help us guard our tongues. In a word: to make us more like Jesus. That is worth it all.

6   *Don't try to end it.* God will do that. As it is put above, 'Don't try to get out of anything prematurely.' This implies that there is a time-scale to every trial. It will last as long as it is supposed to last. Try to end it and you will fail. God will end it. Our assignment is to dignify the trial by letting it run its course, however long God decides that will be. He knows the end from the beginning. Furthermore, when we try to hasten its end prematurely, we forfeit the grace that God intended to bestow on us. A great grace comes to us by *dignifying* the trial, not by trying to abort it. The God who started it will stop it. If we do nothing to bring about its conclusion, but instead let God do that, we will not only have passed the test, but will enjoy the fruit of righteousness that God purposed for us. Speaking personally, I hate to think of how much grace I forfeited over the years by not letting a trial complete its own time. I was forty-four years old when I came to terms with this teaching and began to apply it. It grieves me to think how much I missed, and how many times I failed the test, over the years. I repeat: the trial will end. Do not raise a little finger to make it stop. Let God do this so that you derive the *full* benefit of this source of grace.

7   *Don't grumble.* It is a sobering thought that God puts
    grumbling alongside idolatry and sexual sin in the lists
    of evil deeds that brought his wrath down on ancient
    Israel (1 Cor. 10:1–12). We may look at sexual morality,
    for example, with a very pious horror, but overlook our
    own constant complaining without any pang of con-
    science! We can complain constantly and apparently
    never feel the slightest sense of having grieved the
    Holy Spirit. I can tell you, were we to see how much
    God abhors murmuring and complaining, it would
    get our attention and change our words and attitude.
    Sexual purity passes the test of temptation; gracious-
    ness without grumbling passes the test of the severe
    trial. It takes no talent or training to be able to criticise
    and complain. It is part of being a sinner. It takes great
    grace to endure the hard times and keep quiet about
    them.

8   *Know that God wants you to pass the test far more than you
    do.* There are two reasons for this. First, he loves us *so
    much* and rejoices to see us experience pure joy. Second,
    it brings glory to him when we dignify the trial by
    cheerfully enduring. The angels are watching. As Josif
    Tson once said, 'When God permitted the devil to
    bring calamity to Job, the angels were observing to see
    whether Job would love God without prosperity. For it
    was a testimony to the glory of God for the angels to
    see Job not caving in to questioning God in such a time
    as that. This is why the angels waited with baited breath
    to see Job's reaction. God's honour was at stake in the
    heavenlies as well as on earth. For it brings great glory

to God when he sees one of his children dignifying his trial for them rather than complaining.'

And what if we fail the test? Like it or not, the answer is: we will have to undergo another test later on. One problem is, it may be a while before God trusts us with another test like the one we just failed. In fact, there may never be another quite like it and you will always wish with all your heart you had passed that one. And it may be a while before you even have the equivalent trial. When it comes to failing an exam (like passing a driving test), you may be able to re-take it soon. But the trials God gives are not like that, and this is why we should grasp every trial that God sends with both hands and dignify them.

I remember the following incident as though it were yesterday. Scotland Yard phoned me one afternoon to inform us that our American driving licences were invalid for Great Britain. This meant that it was illegal for us to drive. 'Don't even let your car roll one foot,' the man said quite firmly. The news came only minutes before Louise was due to drive to our children's school to pick them up. Everything had already gone wrong in our house that day. The phone call from Scotland Yard could not have come at a worse time. I said to Louise, 'Either what I preach is true or it isn't. I believe it is true. God has given us a trial at this time and I intend to dignify it. We may never have another like it.' For the next few months we had to be driven everywhere that either of us went. And we had to learn to drive! Never mind that I had been driving since I was sixteen years old, and both of us had been driving all over England for the previous three or four years! But that is the way it was; to have driving licences we had to take tests and learn from a driving instructor before we could take the tests. My friend Dr Lewis Drummond, a pilot who came over from America to teach at Spurgeon's College, told me that it was easier to get a pilot's licence in America than to get a driving licence in England! That episode in our lives made the incident at the pizza shop look like strawberries and cream!

For if we pass the test – like going from A levels to university – there will be a grander opportunity down the road. Since we don't always get another test soon, then, we should take each trial as a special opportunity that will not be repeated in the same way.

Dignifying the trial is done by faith. When Paul tells us to rejoice (Phil. 4:4) it is almost certainly because we don't feel like rejoicing. Otherwise, there was no need for him to say it. The Philippians were not rejoicing because at that time there was a split in the church between two powerful women (Phil. 4:2ff). Paul's initial counsel to them was: 'Rejoice in the Lord always. I will say it again: Rejoice!' You don't do it because you feel like it, you do it in faith. Faith is trusting in God without empirical evidence, only his word. God likes that. If we have the empirical, objective evidence (as we often do have once the trial is over) and *then* rejoice, our response does not qualify as *faith*. Faith is believing without seeing. To the worldly person, seeing is believing. 'Let this Christ, this King of Israel, come down now from the cross, that we may see and believe' (Mark 15:32). That is always the order for the unregenerate person, seeing first – then believing. But it is *not* true faith when that order is followed. Faith is when you believe without the evidence and can say, with Job, 'Though he slay me, yet will I hope in him' (Job 13:15).

To put it another way, once the trial is over and we see for ourselves that this trial worked together for good, little if any faith is required. For that is seeing. Faith is being certain of 'what we do not see' (Heb. 11:1). When we see that there was a purpose in the trial that just ended, our outlook is not graced with the title 'faith'. But when we are in the heat of it and it isn't over yet – and we are dignifying it – that is *faith* at work. It is what pleases God (Heb. 11:6).

There is one more important ingredient for counting a trial 'pure joy'. It is when we 'fall' into the trial, as it is put in the Authorised Version. Whereas the New International Version of the Bible says we 'face' trials, the Authorised Version says to count it all joy when we *fall* into such. The Greek *peripto* can mean that we did nothing to precipitate the trial. It is used in Luke 10:31 where a man going from Jerusalem to Jericho 'fell' into the hands of robbers. It is used in Acts 27:21 to show that the ship ran aground. The point is, we must not go looking for trials. This is one reason Jesus told us to pray that we would not enter into temptation (or trial) (Matt. 6:13; 26:41). If pure joy is the ultimate consequence of dignifying the trial, we may logically conclude that we must go looking for fiery trials! Wrong. The qualification for the trial to be dignified is that we 'fall' into it – it happened without our doing a thing to precipitate it. But when that does happen – and it came along without our causing it – count it *pure joy.* And do not forget, you may never have another trial that is exactly like the one you are now in. Dignify it. You will be glad you did.

And never forget this principle: the greater the suffering, the greater the anointing.

2

The Path to Joy

> No discipline seems pleasant at the time, but painful. Later
> on, however, it produces a harvest of righteousness and peace
> for those who have been trained by it. (Hebrews 12:11)

In August 1956 I fell across the bed in my grandmother's
house in near despair. I cried out 'Why?' Everything seemed
to have gone wrong and the future was bleak. Several months
prior to that I was in an era of what I thought was intimacy
with God and a time of clear revelations that I took to be of
the Holy Spirit. That era lasted for several months, but all
that seemed to collapse in a matter of a few weeks. My
grandmother took the car back she had bought for me over
a year before; my father was crushed in his spirit when he
said I was changing theologically and in church affiliation.
One relative deemed me to be a disgrace to the family, and
I had nothing to show that I was in God's will. On top of

that, a tent meeting that we hoped would bring revival came to nothing only days before it was due to start. 'Why, Lord?' I pleaded, for those visions that came in the preceding months indicated that I would have an international ministry and a very bright future.

I felt an impulse to turn to Hebrews 12:6. I did not know what it said until I turned to it. It read: 'For whom the Lord loveth he chasteneth, and scourgeth every son whom he receiveth' (AV). That was my introduction to the doctrine of chastening, or disciplining, as many modern versions prefer to call it. I had never thought of this concept before, but from then on it became paramount in my quest for more knowledge of God and his word, and it eventually became absolutely essential to all I have taught and preached for the past forty-six years. I cannot imagine a single book I have written that does not refer to God's chastening, either explicitly or implicitly. If I deleted this teaching from the content of my books, they would be in shreds. And yet this is the first time I have devoted so much attention to this subject in a single chapter.

The word we are dealing with comes from the verb *paideuo* – to discipline. The noun is *paideia*. We get the word 'paediatrician' from this family of words, for the *paidion* means 'child'. The meaning of the word used in Hebrews 12:5–11 is *enforced learning*. It partly means punishment, but also correction. The word translated 'scourge' certainly refers to what is painful. But this chastening of the Lord is not him getting even with us for something we did that was wrong, but rather getting us ready. Yes, God may have to deal with us for our misdeeds, but not to the extent that he gets satisfaction from punishing us. God got even at the cross! '. . . as far as the east is from the west, so far has he removed our transgressions from us' (Ps. 103:12). The blood of Jesus did for God's justice what chastening us could never do.

Chastening, or being disciplined, is essentially *preparation*. It will bear repeating: it is not God getting even, but getting us ready. In a word: he chastens us because he has not finished with us yet. Hebrew Christians in the first century seemed to have overlooked an ancient teaching in the Old Testament:

> My son, do not despise the LORD's discipline and do not resent his rebuke, because the LORD disciplines those he loves, as a father the son he delights in. (Proverbs 3:11–12; also Hebrews 12:5–6)

Those Christian Jews were very discouraged at the time. There were several reasons for this. First, many of their friends were no longer attending church services and the numbers of those who did were dwindling (Heb. 10:25). Do you know what it is like to attend the same church for a long time and get to know the people well – only to notice that so many of them have stopped coming? You miss them. You wonder what is wrong. You wonder if *you* are being foolish because you keep coming to the services. We all need fellowship. The best friends are made among those who are converted to the Lord Jesus Christ. But when they become so discouraged that they stop coming to church, it discourages you too. This apparently was happening in the group the writer was addressing in the verses above. Some good commentators would say that such people had never actually been converted in the first place. They base this on 1 John 2:19 ('They went out from us, but they did not really belong to us . . .'). But 1 John 2:19 is not referring to genuine believers here, but to the Gnostics who had wormed their way into the church and were never converted (see Jude 4). The Jews being referred to in the epistle to the Hebrews were not the same at all – they were converted.

Another reason why these people were discouraged was the fact that God had – up until then – withheld vindication from them. The withholding of vindication is a very painful thing to endure. It is when you have been falsely accused, and you long to have your name cleared. You want others – especially your friends – to see clearly that you got it right and were not wrong after all. Those Jews who professed Jesus Christ as their Lord and Messiah were in a minority in the first place, but numbers were now smaller than ever when one looked at the people who attended regularly. So if you were in this ever-increasing minority you felt all the more exposed as seeming very stupid for hanging in there. There was one thing that Jews referred to in order to show that they had got it right and not wrong – namely, Jesus's teaching that the temple would be destroyed (Matt. 24:1–2; Luke 19:41–4). They could say to their fellow Jews, 'Just you wait – you'll see for yourselves – the temple will be destroyed and that will show that we are vindicated for proclaiming that Jesus is the Messiah.' But it was now in the early AD 60s and temple worship thrived in Jerusalem. There was no hint at all that God's judgement had come upon Israel. (This is one proof that Hebrews was written before AD 70 because that is when the temple *was* destroyed by Caesar.) The writer of Hebrews stepped in to address these discouraged Christians and introduced the concept that Jesus was our great high priest (Heb. 4:14) in order to keep them steady.

God was hiding his face from them. They were asking, 'Is it worth it?' This is also why the writer cautions them not to do what some did, namely, they fell away to such a degree that they became stone deaf to the Holy Spirit and could not be renewed to repentance or changed from glory to glory (Heb. 5:11–6:6; 2 Cor. 3:18). He urges them to hold on: 'You have come too far to turn back now,' he virtually tells them (see Heb. 10:32ff), and then exhorts: 'So do not throw away your confidence; it will be richly rewarded' (Heb. 10:35).

This passage was intended to be one of the most encouraging sections in the entire epistle. In essence, he is telling them 'it won't be long now' – God is about to step in. Referring to Habakkuk 2:1–5, the writer says, 'He who is coming will come and will not delay' (Heb. 10:37). Do not give up! God will manifest himself shortly! As the psalmist put it, '. . . weeping may remain for a night, but rejoicing ['joy' in the AV] comes in the morning' (Ps. 30:5).

So whatever is going on in the meantime, says the writer, this much is clear: you are being disciplined by the Lord. The path to joy is one of being chastened. God is teaching you a lesson. You will learn this lesson! For chastening is enforced learning. As to why God was not chastening those other Hebrew Christians – since they too were saved – will become clear below when we look at three types of chastening.

Chastening ain't fun (if I may be excused the bad grammar!). The writer of Hebrews acknowledges this. (Surprise, surprise!) 'No discipline seems pleasant at the time, but painful. Later on, however, it produces a harvest of righteousness and peace for those who have been trained by it' (Heb. 12:11). The Authorised Version says, 'No chastening for the present seemeth to be joyous' (Greek *chara*, 'of joy'). For the path to joy is not always one of joy.

Therefore what James calls falling into trials – which we are to consider pure joy – the writer of Hebrews calls being disciplined, which leads to pure joy. Falling into trials or temptation is what God permits, but still by his sovereign design; being chastened is what God does – all because we are loved.

There is an implicit ground of assurance in this doctrine of chastening. It is an evidence that you are truly saved because the Lord disciplines those he *loves and punishes, those he accepts as a son or daughter* (Heb. 12:6). The writer goes on to talk about illegitimate children who are not true sons or daughters (Heb. 12:8). The way you know you are a true child of God is that you experience this unpleasant thing called chastening. So we could use this syllogism for those who may want to apply it:

1   All who are saved are disciplined, sooner or later (thesis).

2 But I am being disciplined (antithesis).

3 Therefore I am a true child of God (conclusion).

There is an important qualification to the above reasoning – namely, that it works to get your attention, and so you are led to a greater degree of holiness. Otherwise, any person who experiences something unpleasant may glibly conclude that he or she must be a genuine Christian. The syllogism applies only if such painful circumstances result in you seeking the Lord all the more.

The primary purpose of chastening is not to give assurance, but to get our attention. God wants to bring us to holiness, Christ-likeness, intimacy with God, peace and joy. God disciplines us when there is a need for him to have to resort to whatever it is that gets our attention. We may think that he already has our fixed and undivided attention, but if the storm continues, I am sorry to have to say that he does not have our attention as he wants it. As Jack Taylor says, 'If the problem has not been solved or the painful situation has not lifted, it can only mean we have not yet had God's final word on the matter. Any continuing trial means there is work to be done that cannot be accomplished any other way.'

God is a jealous God. Jealousy is a quality we detest in others (and seldom admit to in ourselves), but, like it or not, this is the way God is. He is 'up front' about it and makes no attempt to hide his jealousy. 'I, the LORD your God, am a jealous God' (Exod. 20:5). And if that weren't enough, he adds that his very 'name is Jealous' (Exod. 34:14)! But the crucial differences between the jealousy that is in us and

God's jealousy is: (1) our jealousy is a symptom of insecurity, but God is never insecure; and (2) our jealousy is almost always counter-productive, yet God's jealousy leads to joy. God loves us so much that he wants us to have joy, and that is one of the great reasons that his jealousy is so good for us. Never resent the fact that he is jealous! It is for our good.

The funny thing is (you may want to call it another irony) that what God uses to get our attention may be the very thing that puts us off him! You would think he would use a method or technique that makes him more loveable – or at least more likeable; but often he seems to do the very thing that he must know is making him look pretty awful in our eyes at that moment. It is when he appears to betray us. It is when he seems to turn his back on us. He makes us feel rejected – as though he has dropped us from his good list entirely. It is when he seems disloyal and comes through to us (as best we can tell at the time) as an enemy, not a friend. But Martin Luther used to say that we must know God as an enemy before we can know him as a friend.

To put the purpose of chastening another way, it is given to us that we might *break the betrayal barrier*. It is what few Christians (in my opinion) manage to do, at least, at first – and some, sadly, never succeed. It is one stupendous achievement. When aviation broke the sound barrier (when a supersonic jet flew faster than the speed of sound) it was a tremendous breakthrough. The result of this was that you could fly Concorde (if you could afford it) and, going westbound, leave London at 10 a.m. in the morning and arrive in New York before 9 a.m. the same morning.

But there is a breakthrough that God wants of you and

me – one that is equally awesome in the spiritual realm as breaking the sound barrier is in aviation – and that is one that will put us squarely on the path to joy. It is to break the betrayal barrier in our relationship with God.

All disciplining that comes from our heavenly Father has at bottom the hiding of his face. If you haven't experienced it, I may have to tell you that you are probably not a Christian at all. If indeed you are a child of God, but haven't experienced the hiding of his face, it is only a matter of time. I say that because we are told, '. . . he punishes everyone he accepts' as a son or daughter (Heb. 12:6).

I have been fascinated for years that the words 'Truly you are a God who hides himself, O God and Saviour of Israel' (Isa. 45:15) are inserted in a context that makes no sense for that statement of Isaiah. There is nothing in the preceding lines that prepares one for those words. They just come abruptly, as if out of the blue – and there they are. But why? Why these words at this place? They are true words; they are important and needed. But why here? I have come up with my own theory: that is precisely the way the hiding of God's face is – it comes unexpectedly and without any warning or apparent reason. *God just does it*. The Westminster Confession calls it the withdrawing of the light of his countenance. There is no warning. We find ourselves enjoying his sweet presence when – without any notice – he seems saliently absent. If only God were to say to us when we are enjoying his power and presence, 'Oh, by the way, next Tuesday afternoon about a quarter-past three you will notice that I am withdrawing the smile of my face from you.' No. Never. The hiding of his face never – ever (to my knowledge) – comes with advance warning. God just does it.

The common denominator of all chastening is the hiding of God's face. And the essence of that is the feeling of being betrayed by him and suddenly treating us like an enemy. The psalmist asked God, 'How long, O LORD? Will you forget me for ever? How long will you hide your face from me?' (Ps. 13:1).

The opposite of the hiding of God's face is the show-ing, or smile, of God's face. Moses gave this benediction to ancient Israel: 'The LORD bless you and keep you; the LORD make his face shine upon you and be gracious to you; the LORD turn his face towards you and give you peace' (Num. 6:24–6). When God shows his face it is absolutely blissful. It is when the Dove of the Holy Spirit comes down and remains for a while. God seems very near. You feel him, can almost see him! You read the Bible with great understanding and without your mind wandering. Prayers seem to get answered quickly. People smile at you, and if they don't, it doesn't bother you too much. It is the feeling of the wind being at your back, giving you a gentle push to get things done and to walk through open doors.

But the hiding of God's face? It is awful. In one of John Newton's hymns he made an attempt to describe the hiding of God's face in these lines:

> How tedious and tasteless the hours when Jesus
>   no longer I see;
> Sweet prospects, sweet birds and sweet flowers
>   have all lost their sweetness to me.

I am not sure I could prove this, but I *think* I could endure *anything* so long as God is showing his face. To quote John Newton again, 'But when I am happy in Him, December's as pleasant as May.' But let him hide his face – and it is no fun. But you will probably already know that as well as I do.

God calls each of us to break the betrayal barrier. Dr James Dobson has a chapter on this in his book *When God Doesn't Make Sense.* It is my experience that sooner or later nearly every Christian – virtually ten out of ten – will find some occasion when he or she feels God has betrayed them. But it is also my pastoral experience that roughly only one in ten will break through the betrayal barrier. This is, of course, very sad. Most people, when God is smiling on them, can worship with jubilation, give cheerfully to his work, sacrifice time and pleasure for him, and be expected to volunteer for any help needed at one's church. But let God appear to betray them, and these same people, I am ashamed to say, indicate a rather different story. Roughly nine out of ten say – not in a sweet or submissive voice, but cynically if not sarcastically – 'Thanks a lot, God.' They feel God has let them down at the most crucial moment. It always seems like that. Such people never discover the joy awaiting them on the other side were they to break through that barrier.

Are you wanting more of God? He invites you to break the betrayal barrier. As I mentioned before, A.W. Tozer used to say that we can have as much of God as we want. I disagreed with that at first. This is because I felt I didn't have as much of God as I wanted! But I have decided that Tozer was right: we *can* have as much of God as we want; but that wanting more of him gets tested – by the betrayal barrier. It comes unexpectedly and at the 'worst' time. It is not my *feeling* of wanting more of God – as when I worship or respond to an inspiring message – that proves I really want more of him; it is how I respond to things that happen to me later on that proves I really want more of him.

It is my observation, then, that perhaps one out of ten people find out what joy awaits them on the other side of the betrayal barrier. Most never know the joy that could be theirs were they to dignify the trial and affirm God's chastening of them by breaking the betrayal barrier. The path to joy is the process of breaking the betrayal barrier.

Why should I write like this if my statistics are not very encouraging? For this reason: you can be that rare person who *does* break the betrayal barrier. I often think of these words: 'From this time many of his disciples turned back and no longer followed him' (John 6:66). This is because they felt let down by him. At the beginning of the chapter, 5,000 people wanted to make him king (John 6:1–15), but after they heard his message they wanted nothing to do with him. Only his closest disciples remained with him. Why shouldn't you and I be like those who stayed with him? Why shouldn't you and I break the betrayal barrier? It is what God wants us to do. We do not have to be with the overwhelming majority of those who serve God only when things are the way they want them to be. I write these lines to challenge you to be in that number who will say with Job, 'Though he slay me, yet will I hope in him' (Job 13:15).

Nearly every person God uses a great deal has this in common: they broke through the betrayal barrier. They almost certainly did this *before* they were mightily used. It is not in the pulpit or on a stage or being seen by thousands when you break the betrayal barrier. It is what happens when you are alone. It happens when you have nobody to comfort you, when you are being misunderstood, when people are pointing the finger at you, when everything seems to go wrong – and yet you say, 'Yes, Lord'. That is when a person proves his or her trustworthiness before God and other people. Some would want to call such a person a sovereign vessel. One must be careful here, though. We are not necessarily talking about a high-profile Christian. A sovereign vessel is a person that God has chosen for a special work. It may or may not mean high profile in the Church, and yet it does mean that that person is special. He or she may be up-front before thousands or behind the scenes as a quiet, self-effacing intercessor. In either case, such a vessel of the Holy Spirit will have had to discover God for his- or herself in the hardest of times. This is so that you will believe in God even if nobody else does. To discover God for yourself means that you believe the Bible and the resurrection of Jesus Christ from the dead even if your hero or mentor denies the faith. And what brings about this kind of maturity is breaking the betrayal barrier.

Mary Magdalene did it. There she was at the cross of Jesus, very likely sobbing her heart out over the events of the previous hours. She must have asked the question 'Why would he let them do this?' for she knew in her heart of hearts that he had sufficient power to stop the whole thing. But Jesus gave no explanation to her and let her wonder. It must have been part of his suffering, too, that he was not permitted to say something to make her feel better. She might have felt like asking him, 'Why did you let them do this?' or 'How could you do this to me?' I only know that she was right there at the scene of the crucifixion when nearly all the disciples forsook him and fled. Jesus did not address her at all, but she stayed until the end.

Mary was rewarded; breaking the betrayal barrier always means reward of some kind. Her reward was that she was the first person Jesus appeared to after he was raised from the dead. Mary Magdalene not only stayed at the cross, but remained at the empty tomb after the disciples had left. It was then that Jesus revealed himself – to her, not them. She was the first. Almost certainly she was referred to in Acts 1:14, which means she was filled with the Spirit on the day of Pentecost. What joy awaited her. She did not know she was breaking a betrayal barrier (this is simply the phrase I have chosen), but that is what was happening. Breaking the betrayal barrier led to pure joy for Mary Magdalene: first, at the empty tomb when she held on to Jesus's feet with indescribable joy, and then the joy from the immediate and direct coming of the Holy Spirit to her at Pentecost.

The great men and women of the Old Testament had in common not only their achievements by faith (as in Heb. 11), but also their breaking of the betrayal barrier. It is what Job did. It is what the three Hebrew men did when they refused to bow down to the king's image of gold (Dan. 3) and what Daniel did when he kept praying three times a day despite the threat of being thrown into the lions' den (Dan. 6). A close look at the lives of all those described in Hebrews 11 will show that they broke the betrayal barrier.

That is the person who God uses. It was said of Hezekiah, 'God *left* [my italics] him to test him and to know everything that was in his heart' (2 Chr. 32:31). Hezekiah broke the betrayal barrier.

Do you feel that God has left you? Be assured that he has not left you in the absolute sense; it only seems that way. When God hides his face it is not because he has utterly left us; it only feels that way. That is what Hezekiah felt. The writer put it as he did to show that a great man of God, one of Israel's best kings, was tested to the hilt. Are you too being tested? Are you experiencing the hiding of God's face? I say this with all the integrity I have in me: be encouraged. God is calling you to pure joy. You therefore must follow those who went through the equivalent kind of testing before they could be used to the full and for their potential to be realised. They broke the betrayal barrier. You can do it as well. '. . . no-one has heard, no ear has perceived, no eye has seen' what God will do for those who wait for him (Isa. 64:4; 1 Cor. 2:9).

One of my favourite stories about Arthur Blessitt (the man who has carried a wooden cross around the world – and holds a place in the *Guinness Book of Records* for the longest walk) is when he was carrying his cross in northern Israel. He had no place to stay for the night, so he found a bench by a bus stop and decided to sleep there. It began to rain and he prayed for the rain to stop. He looked at the rain and said, 'I command the rain to stop in the name of Jesus'. And what do you suppose happened? No, it didn't stop. As soon as Arthur uttered those words, there came a bolt of lightning and a loud crash of thunder and the rain came down harder than ever. Arthur looked up to heaven and said, 'God, I love you anyway.'

Martin Luther stood before the Diet at Worms in 1520 because of his pamphlets. When ordered by the hierarchy to repudiate his tracts, he asked to be given twenty-four hours. It was granted. That night in his cell he prayed. He cried out to God in agony, 'My God, art thou dead? No, thou canst not die; thou only hidest thyself.' One could imagine this would have been an appropriate time for God to honour Luther with a band of angels or a visit by the angel Gabriel. But no. Luther felt nothing and was unaware of any special company. The next day he stood before the authorities. 'Dr Luther, will you deny what you have written in these pamphlets?' they asked. He replied, 'I do if you can show me that they are contrary to the word of God, but if not, here I stand, I can do no other. God help me. Amen.' Luther, again, felt nothing. He was scared; he felt so alone for he stood alone. But it was his finest hour.

Six principles of God's discipline

There are some principles that pertain to the teaching of God's chastening. To grasp these will help to lead you on in your walk along the path to joy:

1 *Being disciplined is inevitable if you are a Christian*. It is only a matter of time before God's chastening, or being disciplined by him, will be our experience. There are no Christians without it. This leads to the following question: does God ever chasten the non-Christian? Yes,

but only if it leads to conversion. God knows his elect before they are converted. He even sends angels to those who *will* be heirs of salvation (Heb. 1:14), which may indicate that they have certain blessings before they are actually converted. Likewise, it should not surprise us if God deals with his people before they are saved in order to get their attention. But as for the non-Christian who will never be saved, no, I would not use the word 'chasten', or 'discipline', which in Hebrews 12 means enforced learning. God may send calamity and even punish them (see Acts 12:23), but one should not call this chastening – a word reserved for the Lord's own people.

2   *Chastening is proof you are a Christian*. '. . . the Lord disciplines those he loves . . . if you are not disciplined (and everyone undergoes discipline), then you are illegitimate children and not true sons' (Heb. 12:6, 8). We saw above that this may in some sense be regarded as a ground of assurance. When God allows pain in your life that results in bringing you to your knees to seek the way of holiness, it is because you are saved. You are loved. Jonah, a type of backslider, was severely chastened. He ended up in the belly of a big fish. God said to him, 'Go to the great city of Nineveh' (Jonah 1:2). God said 'go', Jonah said 'no'. I think that God looked down on Jonah and said, 'Really?' God *could* have finished off Jonah then and there. (He could have done that with any of us, could he not?) But God showed mercy towards Jonah and decided to do exactly what it took to get Jonah's attention. It is kind of funny:

what Jonah refused to do at first he ended up praying earnestly in order to get to do! As we used to sing in the hills of Kentucky, 'He doesn't compel us against our will, but makes us willing to go'. God does that with his own – but only them. Hebrews 12:6–8 proves that God does not discipline everybody because not everybody will be saved. This matter of being disciplined by our heavenly Father is the experience of his children only. For they alone are called to find the path that leads to pure joy.

3 *Being disciplined is from a loving, perfect Father.* 'Moreover, we have all had human fathers who disciplined us and we respected them for it. How much more should we submit to the Father of our spirits and live!'(Hebrews 12:9). The writer interestingly makes a comparison between our parents and the Perfect Parent. None of us had perfect parents. Indeed, they were, or are, quite imperfect. I love my parents (now in heaven), but there is no doubt in my mind that I have suffered considerable damage as a result of my upbringing. I also love our children and they love me; but they too have suffered seriously because of my imperfections. I have shouted at them (God doesn't do that), punished them when I lost my temper (God never does that), or corrected them so that people watching would see that I was not letting my kids get away with this or that (God has nothing he needs to prove – to people or angels). In fact, I have made so many mistakes as a parent that it is the basis for my greatest sense of guilt. But God never feels guilty. He never makes mistakes. He corrects us not so that

people will be impressed by his dealing with us, but only because he loves us. Every single thing he does regarding us is not with the view of looking over his shoulder to see who is watching, but because he does what he does for our good. The greatest freedom is having nothing to prove and God has nothing to prove. He is the Perfect Parent.

4   *Chastening is preparation,* that we may 'share in his holiness' (Heb. 12:10). As I said above, God got even at the cross. He is not playing a game of 'tit for tat'. He disciplines us because there is a future for us. He doesn't chasten yesterday's man or woman. In my book *The Anointing* I try to show that King Saul, a type of yesterday's man, lost his anointing not because of age or retirement, but because he was unteachable and could not be renewed to repentance. Preparation is what God does because he hasn't finished with us yet. Charles Spurgeon said that if he knew he had twenty-five years left to live, he would spend twenty of them in preparation. But God's preparation is to refine us, to make us instruments for 'noble purposes, made holy, useful to the Master and prepared to do any good work' (2 Tim. 2:21). This kind of preparation God calls 'chastening', or being disciplined, because there is more work for us to do – whatever one's age. God did not allow Moses to do the chief work to which he was called until he was eighty. All was preparation up until then. It continued after that as well!

5   *Being disciplined is unpleasant.* It may seem needless to say this again, but the writer of Hebrews makes a point to

state the obvious: 'No discipline seems pleasant at the time, but painful' (Heb. 12:11). I find it comforting to know that the Lord himself realises what it is he is putting us through and knows it isn't fun. Because it does really hurt. When we are either ill or in financial trouble, needing vindication or emotional healing, or are lonely or whatever – and God is hiding his face the whole time – you wonder if you can stand it another day. And then more happens the next day instead of it being lifted. And yet however painful it may be, none of us will ever suffer like Jesus did, nor have we shed blood (Heb. 12:4). The good news is it won't last for ever. God knows how much we can bear, and he will make a way of escape (1 Cor. 10:13). He will step in. It may seem he waited too long, but the truth is, he is never too late, never too early, but always just on time.

6   *His discipline is worth dignifying and the joy that follows is worth it all.* 'Later on, however, it produces a harvest of righteousness and peace for those who have been trained by it' (Heb. 12:11). I will never forget Colin Dye trying to describe to me what he felt when, at his hotel in Brazil, as he stepped from one room to another, he suddenly was seized with an almost overwhelming sense of the presence of God. 'I would have endured anything for that one brief moment,' he said to me. Colin and Amanda Dye have gone through a lot of suffering, far more than most people endure. Their daughter Laura, who recently died at the age of sixteen, never walked or talked and had to wear nappies all her life, and never

knew normality; neither did her parents see her healing that they so earnestly had prayed for. But Colin wanted to explain that those few brief seconds of God's presence – pure joy – were so utterly fulfilling that all he endured seemed as nothing in comparison. This was Paul's point, 'I consider that our present sufferings are not worth comparing with the glory that will be revealed in us' (Rom. 8:18).

God has a work for you to do that nobody can do as well as you can. Your own gift, or anointing, is unique. But if your time has not yet come, it is because there is a little bit more work for God to do in you. Victory Hugo said, 'Like the trampling of a mighty army, so is the force of an idea whose time has come.' If I may paraphrase that, I would say that, like the trampling of a mighty army, 'so is the force of one's anointing whose time has come'. But one has to wait on God's time; and if the disciplining continues, God isn't finished with what we need. As Jack Taylor says, 'If the crisis we have been in continues, or the problem is not yet solved, it means we haven't had God's final word on the matter.' God does not chasten us idly or without reason; it is exactly what we need for the task he has designed for us.

Three kinds of chastening

There are basically three kinds of chastening, or of God's discipline: internal, external and terminal:

1   *Internal chastening.* This is God's primary way of dealing
    with us. It is through his word and it is what God does
    to us from within. It is God's way of trying to get our
    attention via preaching, teaching, hymns, our daily devo-
    tions and through prayer. I call it God's Plan A. It is the
    best way to have our problems solved. If only we would
    listen to him when he speaks! It would spare us a lot of
    problems that could have been avoided. I would urge
    you, when God speaks to you, grasp what he says with
    both hands and with all your heart. It will spare you
    grief later on. Call on him to speak to your heart and
    do what he does best in his own operating theatre. 'For
    the word of God is living and active. Sharper than any
    double-edged sword, it penetrates even to dividing soul
    and spirit, joints and marrow; it judges the thoughts and
    attitudes of the heart' (Heb. 4:12). Internal disci-
    plining, when nobody but *you* knows what God
    is saying, is by far the preferred method of God's
    chastening, and it is the way God begins – by his word.

2   *External chastening.* This is Plan B. It is God's strategy
    from outside us – as in losing your job, financial reverse,
    putting you flat on your back, being swallowed by a big
    fish like Jonah, or whatever it takes to get your attention.
    Plan B is what most of us invariably need, and it is
    precisely this that the writer of Hebrews is talking about
    in Hebrews 12:5–11. In other words, what that passage
    describes is what I am calling God's Plan B. When I say
    it is what most of us nearly always get, I can say it is the
    way God certainly has dealt with me. If only I had
    listened when he spoke the first time! When someone

asked me why I chose to preach on the book of Jonah as my first series at Westminster Chapel, I answered: I *am* Jonah. God tried to get my attention via his own word, but I would not listen. It forced him to turn to Plan B before I obeyed as I should have done. I thank God for his Plan B. He did not have to stay with me when I was stubborn, but he did. He did so with Jonah and he has done so with me. How about you?

3   *Terminal chastening.* I pray that you or I will never need this. It is the worst scenario for a person who has truly been saved. This manner of discipline, generally speaking, usually takes one of two forms: (1) physical death, as when Ananias and Saphira lied to the Holy Spirit (Acts 5:1–11); or (2) stone deafness to the Spirit so that one can no longer hear God's voice (Heb. 5:11–6:6). In 1 Corinthians 11 Paul describes those Christians who were weak and sickly (Plan B), but also those who slept – a euphemism for a Christian's death, terminal chastening. Sadly, God calls some home who will not respond positively to Plan B. In other cases, he simply inflicts stone deafness upon them; they become yesterday's men or women and are useless to him in his kingdom, but they are still around.

The path to joy is submitting to God's Plan A or his Plan B. This will mean breaking the betrayal barrier. There is a way, though, to break the betrayal barrier.

How to break the betrayal barrier

1 Affirm from your heart that what is happening is God's idea. What is designed to get your attention may put you off, yes, but it is God's idea to do it this way. His ways are higher than our ways and his thoughts are higher than our thoughts (Isa. 55:8–9). Affirm what he is doing in the heat of the battle. Tell him: 'Lord, I know this is from you, I accept it.' All you really have to say is, 'Yes, Lord'. That will do.

2 Realise this is possibly the greatest opportunity you will ever have to know him intimately:

> Standing somewhere in the shadows you'll find Jesus;
> He's the only one who cares and understands;
> Standing somewhere in the shadows you'll find Jesus,
> And you'll know him by the nail prints in his hands.
>
> *Anonymous*

3 Pray more than ever. Take every available moment to seek his face. Spend every minute you can in secret with him without the television on, or people around who could intrude. I don't mean for you to become a recluse or retreat into a monastery. But when you are in the depth of a severe, fiery trial, this may be the best way forward. Seek him with all your heart. Get to know him and his ways and see if there is anything in particular he may be trying to show you. 'Search me, O God, and know my heart; test me and know my anxious thoughts.

See if there is any offensive way in me, and lead me in the way everlasting' (Ps. 139:23–4).

4   Walk in all the light God gives you. 'But if we walk in the light, as he is in the light, we have fellowship with one another, and the blood of Jesus, his Son, purifies us from all sin' (1 John 1:7). Confess any sin God brings to your attention. Accept any form of new obedience he puts before you. I began the Pilot Light ministry at Westminster Chapel because I had to! I had no other choice. To be totally honest, every measure of obedience I've ever achieved, as I tried to put it in my book *In Pursuit of His Glory*, has been because God gave me no other choice.

Just do what he says! Don't look over your shoulder to get approval or to see if others are doing the same thing; just obey the Lord and never look back. This is the path to pure joy.

3

The Joy of God's Esteem

How can you believe if you accept praise from one another, yet make no effort to obtain the praise that comes from the only God? (John 5:44)

This verse has influenced me, and probably governed me, more than any other verse in the Bible. I have probably quoted it more than any other verse in all my preaching ministry next to Romans 8:28. When someone asks me to sign a book or write my name in their Bible I tend to put Romans 8:28 after my name. I tried using John 5:44 a few times, but it confused people; some thought I was trying to send them a direct message or hint that I thought they needed that verse, so it did not edify them, and I stopped using it for that particular reason. But this *is* the verse that means more to me than any other. If I have an unfulfilled dream when it comes to writing a book, it would be an elaboration of this verse with a very full and detailed study of the glory of God.

The Authorised Version translates this verse, 'How can ye believe, which receive honour one of another, and seek not the honour that cometh from God only?' This suggests that we should seek only the honour of God and that there is an honour that comes from him that is distinct from the honour that comes from people. It is this idea that grips me most – because it indicates a promise that there is a special honour God delights to give to those who esteem it above the praise that comes from people.

Not that I myself have successfully or consistently sought to obtain the honour Jesus had in mind, or that I have even come close to receiving it. Hardly! I can only say that the depth to which this verse stirs me and grips me has left a longing in my heart that is so earnest that I have spent the last forty-five years endeavouring to understand and experience this verse for myself. Perhaps this verse has spoken to me so much simply because I have an acute weakness in wanting people's approval. I have always been convicted by Paul's words, 'Am I now trying to win the approval of men, or of God? Or am I trying to please men? If I were still trying to please men, I would not be a servant of Christ' (Gal. 1:10). This last sentence haunts me – that I might still be trying to please men – and so not be a servant of Christ. If this is true without any conditions or mitigating circumstances, I fear that I have been disqualified from being called a servant of Christ many times. For if I made a list of my greatest weaknesses, I am quite sure that this would be at the very top of the list: I want to please people too much.

None the less, I can say that I have tried hard over the years to exemplify the principles inherent in John 5:44, whether in small things or big things. Small things would refer to fishing for a compliment (when I should wait and let others say what they feel without any hints from me); big things would refer to major decisions at crucial stages in my life (like whether to endorse a controversial ministry or to accept a particular invitation).

It is interesting to note that Jesus did not rebuke the Jews he was addressing because they had not *obtained* the honour of God; he rebuked them because they had *made no attempt* to obtain it. It was not even in their minds to think in this manner. The implication is, they should have done so; they should have known better. Hundreds of years of teaching about the honour and glory of God should have resulted in their seeking it above all else. Indeed, had they been bent on seeking the honour that comes from God, they never would have missed the Messiah in the first place. They missed the Man that God sent to them because it was not a part of their way of thinking or doing things. This is the reason Jesus said, 'How *can* you believe . . . if you make no effort to obtain the praise that comes from the only God?' Not to make an attempt to obtain God's praise is what removes the possibility of true faith. Their seeking the praise of people apparently rendered faith an impossibility in one stroke.

This is a warning and an encouragement to you and me. The warning: if you and I do not make an attempt to receive the praise that comes from God rather than the praise of people, we too will find it impossible to exercise genuine faith. The encouragement: we are not required to have obtained the honour and praise of God, but only to *make an effort* to obtain it. God's commands are not burden-some (1 John 5:3). He is not demanding that we perfectly repudiate the praise of people and absolutely receive his praise; he is only asking us to make an effort to obtain his praise. Nothing can be more reasonable than that.

Jesus therefore asked, 'How *can* you believe . . . ?' if no attempt is made to seek solely the honour of God. The conclusion is: if you are not seeking God's honour but only the praise of people, it is not possible to have true faith. If you seek people's applause rather than God's praise, you render the possibility of believing out of the question, says Jesus. This, then, is how they missed their promised Messiah.

What is so scary about this implication is that you and I could continue to miss what God may be up to in his church generally and in our lives in particular. If I choose the praise of people over God's approval, I will be a victim of unbelief. I will render myself incapable of believing God, as he wants me to. I will likewise miss whatever God has chosen to do at the moment. Jonathan Edwards taught us that the task of every generation is to discover in which direction the Sovereign Redeemer is moving, then move in that direction. But if I am found being enamoured with the praise of people during the time God is at work in my day or in my area, I will miss seeing his glory – even if it is right in front of me. That is what happened to the ancient Jews in Israel and it can happen to us today. I can think of nothing worse than that.

This verse therefore contains an immense encouragement, namely, if I but *seek* – or make an effort to obtain – his honour, I will be able to believe and see what he is up to. That way, I won't miss his activity. I won't miss what he is doing, where he is at work and how he is moving. God has implicitly guaranteed in this verse that if you and I will set as a goal his honour and glory in all our thinking and decision-making, two things will follow: (1) we will be people of genuine faith; and (2) we will see him work – whenever, however, and wherever that may be.

This verse thus contains a promise of joy – a joy that no purer can be conceived. That joy is actually, personally and consciously receiving the praise of God. It is when he esteems me. He affirms me. He approves of me. He lets me know it in a definite way. There is no greater joy on earth than this.

We all grow up wanting parental approval. My desire to excel when I was a small boy in school was motivated almost entirely by the look on my dad's face when he saw my report card. I am not sure I ever outgrew that! During the last seven years of his life he had Alzheimer's disease, but just a year or two before this illness set in, when he was in his eighties, his approval meant the world to me. But how much more do we need our heavenly Father's approval. There is no greater joy to be had on this earth than the conscious awareness of his praise. Nothing compares. It is pure joy.

It was no small thing for Jesus to hear the words, 'This is my Son, whom I love; with him I am well pleased' (Matt. 3:17). That was at Jesus's baptism. Later on, when he was transfigured before Peter, James and John, he used the same words again, 'This is my Son, whom I love; with him I am well pleased. Listen to him!' (Matt. 17:5). These words thrilled Jesus to his fingertips. It is all he wanted to hear; to know he was pleasing his Father. That is all he lived for.'. . . I always do what pleases him' (John 8:29). This is what gave him joy.

It is what will give us joy as well. Pure joy. The best feeling in the world. The most satisfying and fulfilling feeling in the world. It means a good conscience. It means you are walking in the light (1 John 1:7). It means God can use you. It means you won't miss anything he may want to do in your life and that you will be 'in' on it should he be pleased to move in your time. You won't be left out. All he envisages for you will be yours.

None of us wants to be a 'has been' – or a yesterday's man or woman. A horrible spiritual position is to be in a place where you can't hear God speak any more (Heb. 5:11–6:6) or where you cannot be changed from glory to glory any more (2 Cor. 3:18). But when you have God's definite praise and approval, believe me, that is as good as it gets. You know you haven't missed what God wants to do with you and that he can put you anywhere he pleases. Of course, because he is sovereign and all-powerful, he can put anybody anywhere he pleases – regardless of whether they have been pursuing his glory. But the *promise* of experiencing this honour is given to those who maintain good communication with him. I wish that all of us in his family did this.

The word 'esteem' means to think highly of; it means respect or favourable opinion. Can anything be more fantastic than to have God esteem you – to think highly of you? This, it seems to me, is somewhat different from love. It is wonderful to be loved by God, but God loves the world

(John 3:16). God moreover loves all his people – his elect – with a particularity and security that is not the same as for those who are not his. Likewise, being esteemed by God suggests that one is not only loved by him, because you are a member of the family, but that you are honoured in a special way that not all in the family enjoy.

God said to Gideon, 'The LORD is with you, mighty warrior' (Judg. 6:12). Three times the Lord said to Daniel, 'You are highly esteemed' (Dan. 9:23; 10:11, 19). Moses and Abraham had in common that each was called God's friend (Exod. 33:11; Isa. 42:8). God said of Hezekiah, 'There was no-one like him among all the kings of Judah, either before him or after him' (2 Kgs. 18:5). God did not say this of every king, because not every king was obedient as Hezekiah was. God said of Josiah, 'Neither before nor after Josiah was there a king like him who turned to the LORD as he did – with all his heart and with all his soul and with all his strength, in accordance with the Law of Moses' (2 Kgs. 23:25). King David was called a man after God's own heart (1 Sam. 13:14; Acts 13:22). The fact that a man as vulnerable as David could be called that shows us that perfection is not required to have God's esteem! No human being on earth is without sin: '. . . there is no-one who does not sin' (1 Kgs. 8:46). Sinless perfection has never existed except in the person of Jesus Christ (Heb. 4:15).

What is required of us is not perfection, but *seeking* – making an effort to obtain – his praise and esteem. It must be something you want in your heart of hearts. It must be pre-eminently important to you. It must regulate your life and the decisions you make. What is the reward? Pure joy.

How much time and energy is required on our part? It all depends. If we *want* his esteem, it follows that we are going to walk in any ray of light he gives to us along the way. We prove we want his esteem by the decisions we make. The honour of God is therefore at our fingertips. It is closer than our hands or our feet, closer than the air we breathe. It is centred in the mind, heart and will. In the mind, that we perceive the difference between the praise of people and the commendation of God. In the heart, that we sincerely want his honour and approval more than we want anything in this world. In the will, that we demonstrate what we say we want in our hearts by what we say when faced with the temptation to desire earthly praise more than we want his smile. One could say, therefore, that to have the esteem of God is the easiest thing in the world to achieve because he is eager to show it. And yet to feel that esteem and hear his 'well done' comes to those who show that it is really what they want by their words and deeds.

God had already esteemed Israel. The Jews were special. They were the primary object of God's affections. God has always had a 'soft spot' for Israel, but they had developed a preference for the praise of one another. This is why Jesus asked them, 'How can you believe if you accept praise from one another, yet make no effort to obtain the praise that comes from the only God?' They accepted praise from one another because this was where their hearts were. '. . . for they loved praise from men more than praise from God' (John 12:43). Jesus said of them, 'Everything they do is done for men to see' (Matt. 23:5). This is why they announced their almsgiving with trumpets – 'to be honoured by men' (Matt. 6:2). They prayed in public for the same reason (Matt. 6:5), and it is what motivated them to fast (Matt. 6:16). The concept of doing these things utterly and totally for God alone was not something they apparently even considered. This, then, is why they could not believe, and this unbelief was the bottom line in their failing to spot the Messiah.

It is a powerful and wonderful thing to have God's esteem. This is possible not because of our profile, our importance or performance, but because we want it more than anything else. This means that *you* – whoever you are – can have God's esteem. You don't have to be Daniel the prophet. Daniel was called highly esteemed not because he was a prophet, but because he loved God more than the approval of people (Dan. 6:10). It was his love for God's honour that put him where he was; he could be trusted with a high profile *because* it meant less to him than God's honour.

You or I may not be given the privilege to prophesy before royalty or heads of state, but we can be just as esteemed by the Father as Daniel was. Profile does not mean that God is pleased with you. There are people who are rich and famous, but they will never experience God's commendation. All that is required is to want it – more than anything. That's all. Our acts and words will prove that we really want it.

Therefore high profile on earth has nothing to do with receiving God's esteem in heaven. You can be royal or a head of state and never get it, an ambassador and never get it, a merchant banker or a wealthy stockbroker and never know God's 'well done'. For these things mean little in heaven. Jesus went so far as to say that, 'What is highly valued among men is detestable in God's sight' (Luke 16:15). Of course, this does not mean that if you are royal or a head of state, you will *not* have the knowledge of God's esteem. God loves to show his approval to all people. But it has nothing to do with their position or earthly prestige. It has all to do with their preference for his applause rather than that of men and women.

If you say that you really do want the knowledge of his esteem more than you want the praise of people, I can give you a prophecy I know will be fulfilled! My prophecy to you is, you will have an opportunity *soon* – very soon – to show which means more to you: people's praise or God's praise of you. Do not be surprised if my prophecy to you is fulfilled before another day passes!

Let me list the possible ways my word to you may be fulfilled:

1 Credit

Who gets the credit? Can you do something good or worth-while and keep quiet about it? What if you do something heroic, sacrificial or valiant and nobody notices? What if someone does know about it, but even he or she says or does nothing to ensure you get sufficient commendation? It may 'get your goat' or hurt you deeply. But can you hold your peace and control your tongue?

Can you be content with the knowledge 'God knows'? In other words, would his knowledge of what you did be enough for you? Or do you say to yourself, 'I know God knows, but surely I deserve to have someone around me to

70

be aware of what I did?' I sympathise with you if that is your thinking. I've been there a thousand times, and it hurts.

But this is precisely where we show how much God's esteem means. What if God says that you cannot have it both ways; you have to choose between knowing he knows and having the admiration of people? Sometimes we *can* have it both ways, providing we made the choice for his glory. What if you have to wait until you get to heaven before people have the true picture, is that OK with you? If so, you're *there*; that is the goal you and I must reach: the willingness to wait until we get to heaven to get proper recognition.

And yet God does step in sometimes before we get to heaven. He did so with Mordecai who saved the life of the king, but only got due recognition because one night the king couldn't sleep and happened to notice all that happened (Esther 2:22–3; 6:1–14). When we don't sound our trumpets, exercise our pious duties so they are seen, and keep quiet when we have done something good, God notices. He *will* demonstrate his esteem; sometimes here below, sometimes at the final judgement. We must come to the place, though, where it doesn't matter very much which it is. On President Ronald Reagan's desk in the Oval Office was a plaque that read: 'There is no limit to how far a person can go as long as he doesn't care who gets the credit for it'. I do not know the origin of the statement, but it is quite profound and reflects the principles of John 5:44.

But must we wait until we get to heaven to experience pure joy? Not at all. When we desire God's sole approval so much, and resist the temptation to forfeit that approval by not caving in to the need for people's admiration, it is a triumph of grace. Sometimes it is but an inner peace that you did the right thing – but so satisfying because you realise you have proved how much God's sole commendation meant to you. When you can hear him say 'I know' and you treasure that more than gold, you have experienced what the Jews of Jesus's day knew nothing about.

I don't mean to be unfair, but if you do not experience this joy in the knowledge that God alone knows and is pleased with you, it may be because his esteem is not valued very much yet. For example, if you do the right thing – keep quiet rather than tell what you did, but don't do it very cheerfully – you may feel resentment instead of joy. It is like giving, or tithing. If you give one-tenth to the Lord, but are upset at having to turn loose that money that could have been used elsewhere, God is not pleased with the money you gave. This is why Paul said, 'Each man should give what he has decided in his heart to give, not reluctantly or under compulsion, for God loves a cheerful giver' (2 Cor. 9:7). The principle involved when seeking the honour of God is exactly the same. When you really want this more than anything, it is pure joy when you discover you didn't give in to the temptation of desiring people's applause. But if you control your tongue half-heartedly and feel cheated that people aren't going to know what you did, you will not experience pure joy. It comes when you value God's esteem above the esteem of those who matter to you.

Getting the credit for having done the right thing is called vindication. It is a good feeling. It is often an ego thing; we all love it. But Jesus was 'vindicated by the Spirit'

(1 Tim. 3:16). It is the Holy Spirit's immediate and direct witness that Jesus had the Father's esteem. He was hated by the people he initially came to save; he came unto his own, but his own did not receive him (John 1:11). He knew what it was to be hated (John 15:18), but he got his joy from knowing he always pleased the Father – and that was vindication enough for Jesus. That is why it is called vindication by the Spirit. Not vindication by the people. But only by the Spirit. We too may experience this. In fact, it is one of the ways that pure joy is experienced. It is the Holy Spirit witnessing directly to you that you have pleased your heavenly Father. It is a sublime experience that God wants for each of us.

2 Credibility

What if your reputation is under a cloud? This, of course, refers to the withholding of vindication. It is when people no longer believe in you: they do not trust you and you have lost credibility with them. It hurts a lot. But Jesus has been there too. In the early part of John 6 he had to escape the crowds because they were determined to make him king (John 6:14–15), but in the end they didn't believe in him at all (John 6:66)! Jesus lost credibility in their eyes.

God has an amazing way of causing us to lose credibility – to get our attention and make us want his opinion. When everyone believes in us and wants to 'crown' us, it is not so easy to value God's approval of us. But when they back away and distance themselves from us, we are more likely to seek the praise that comes only from him. For that reason, he lets situations and circumstances develop in such a way that we are driven to our knees to seek his face.

What causes us to lose credibility will largely be (1) what we believe, and (2) those we associate with. When what we believe is unfamiliar territory to our friends, they quietly tiptoe away and we wake up one day with the realisation that these people aren't behaving in the same way towards us. For the first five years of our ministry at Westminster Chapel I was very popular with my members and many in our constituency, but after I invited Arthur Blessitt in, and we went out into the streets with the gospel (our Pilot Light ministry), and began singing choruses and inviting people to come forward at the end of the evening services, one by one my old support dwindled. I lost credibility with these people. My theology did not change, but I believed we needed to emphasise evangelism more and loosen up a bit! My invitations to preach that previously came from our constituency ended abruptly.

What kept me sane in those days? One thing and one thing alone: I knew I was obeying the Holy Spirit and that the honour of God's name was at stake. I knew I had his approval and so we coped, although it was very hard. Losing the support of the same people who voted you in to be their minister is pretty tough. I got my joy not from without, but from within. Pure joy.

A verse that has come to be precious to me in this connection is Hebrews 13:13, 'Let us, then, go to him outside the camp, bearing the disgrace he bore.' Going outside the camp means to leave the traditional structures or establishment, the way of thinking that is common to you and your friends (or enemies), and even the people who may be hopelessly conservative. It is leaving them behind, and that is a painful thing to do. Those Hebrew Christians probably had it much tougher than anything you or I will have to endure. They were in turmoil. They broke from an ancient tradition that preceded them by over 1,300 years; they were also outnumbered by tens of thousands of Jews who stuck with the traditional way of worship. Talk about leaving your comfort zone! They really did this, and those who went outside the camp lost all credibility. They were reminded by the writer of Hebrews, however, that all they were doing was following Jesus who, as it happened, suffered on the cross outside the city of Jerusalem (Heb. 13:12).

As for those days in Westminster Chapel, it got worse! The day would come, though, when a Paul Cain or a Rodney Howard-Browne would make Arthur Blessitt seem like a harmless conservative Christian! So our pilgrimage outside the camp continued. I have been fascinated by Paul Cain's comment, 'The further out the better'. Not all would agree. But what matters if the honour of God is at stake? It is his opinion that matters – nothing more. The Greek word *doxa* (glory) comes from a root word that means 'opinion'. The glory of God is his opinion. No matter how far outside the camp someone feels he must go, the awareness of God's smile compensates for it all. It is indeed pure joy, even when you lose credibility.

But a caution is in order. Peter warned that we must be sure that any suffering is for doing what is right, not what is wrong. 'But how is it to your credit if you receive a beating for doing wrong and endure it?' (1 Pet. 2:20). Likewise, some may go outside the camp who are either heretics or complete weirdos! They do the cause of God no good at all, even though they think they are being persecuted for righteousness. I cannot go into the issue here of what makes a heretic a heretic, or a weirdo a weirdo, only to say that if your doctrine is orthodox and your motive is the honour of God, you will come out smelling like a rose at the end of the day – plus experiencing the joy of the Lord. Moreover, sometimes (perhaps not very often, but it does happen) the very people who once scorned you will meekly say to you, 'I'm sorry, I got it wrong.' You forgive them and move on. And if that doesn't happen, you still forgive them and move on! Live by Paul's way of applying John 5:44, which is found in his candid remarks to his beloved church at Corinth:

I care very little if I am judged by you or by any human court; indeed, I do not even judge myself. My conscience is clear, but that does not make me innocent. It is the Lord who judges me. Therefore judge nothing before the appointed time; wait till the Lord comes. He will bring to light what is hidden in darkness and will expose the motives of men's hearts. At that time each will receive his praise from God. (1 Cor. 4:3–5)

3 Contentment

This means being content with the praise that comes only from God and not trying to have it both ways (the praise of God *and* people). Contentment with the honour or praise that comes only from God means several things: (1) keeping quiet about that which would make yourself look good;

(2) never complaining or grumbling over hardships or suffering; (3) doing nothing, not even raising a little finger, to hasten vindication.

There is an old spiritual that comes from the cotton fields of the Deep South in America that says, 'Nobody knows the troubles I've seen, nobody knows but Jesus'. Contentment with the honour of God alone means that you are happy for Jesus to be the only one who knows. It feels good when we can share our weeping or rejoicing with others, and there is a time and place for both, or the Bible would not say, 'Rejoice with those who rejoice; mourn with those who mourn' (Rom. 12:15). But there is also the challenge to let *only* Jesus weep with you, or rejoice with you. He may ask this of us to test us, to see which means more to us: his awareness of what we've been through, or those we know being aware of such.

The contentment that is implied in the praise that comes only from God is of two kinds: (1) the direct witness of the Spirit by which God immediately rewards us for making the right choice; or (2) when you feel nothing whatsoever from him, but know in your heart you made the right choice – and feel good about it without being self-righteous.

Our Lord Jesus, who possessed the Spirit without any limit (John 3:34), got his joy from the Father and not from the affirmation of people. When he asked the disciples, 'Who do people say the Son of Man is?' (Matt. 16:13), he was not trying to build up his ego or self-esteem – he knew exactly what people thought about him. He was getting them to think for themselves. But when you and I ask, 'What did so-and-so say about me?' or 'Did they mention me?', it is almost certainly a sign of our insecurity. The more we are filled with the Spirit (although we will never have the Spirit without measure here on earth), the more we will be content with the praise and honour that comes only from God.

I sometimes ask people, 'Could you have tea with Her Majesty the Queen and keep quiet about it?' Better still, 'Do you think you could turn down an honour from the Queen and keep quiet about it?' I knew of a man who – to everyone's surprise – accepted a knighthood from the Queen and was asked why he accepted it. The man replied, 'Nobody should turn down a knighthood without keeping quiet about it and I knew I couldn't, so I accepted it.' The power of the ego is usually too much for us not to share things like this. According to Ecclesiastes 4:4, all achievements spring from the desire to have people envy us or to stand in awe of us.

At the spiritual level how many of us can have an unusual experience with God and not tell someone else about it? Some experiences with the Lord, though, are meant to be told because they can have the effect of making others hungry for more of God. In this case, therefore, telling of an experience with God honours him. But some experiences with the Lord are *not* to be told because they only serve to make us look good. As a consequence, many of us never have extraordinary experiences with God because we would not be able to resist the temptation to tell others about them. This may be why the psalmist said that the 'secret' of the Lord is with them who fear him (Ps. 25:14, AV) since the Lord apparently does not confide in everybody.

I will never forget one lady – who apparently had minimal

objectivity about herself – who came to our table in a restaurant to tell us how she had spent much time that week visiting those who were house-bound. I commended her, whereupon she added: 'The joy is in not telling it.' In one stroke she forfeited the praise from God.

The person who is content with God's esteem alone, and who will not knowingly seek the applause of people, is rare in this world. But it is a challenge from our Lord that we must accept because the joy that follows is better than what people's praise can do for us.

4

Rejoicing in the Lord

Finally, my brothers, rejoice in the Lord! . . . Rejoice in the Lord always. I will say it again: Rejoice (Philippians 3:1; 4:4)

The book of Philippians has been called 'an epistle of joy'. This is mainly because of the repeated use of the Greek word *chara* – 'joy' – used five times in the epistle, and *chairo* – 'rejoice' – eleven times. There are two ironies in this connection between rejoicing and this letter to the Philippians: (1) there was little evidence for any rejoicing among the believers at Philippi at that time; and (2) Paul himself had no external cause for rejoicing in those days. He was in prison as he wrote and was being persecuted by fellow Christian ministers!

The reason someone is given a command is usually because the person receiving the command needs it, and would be unlikely to do what is commanded without that command. Paul puts the exhortation to rejoice in the imperative mood. The Philippians must have needed it or he would not have commanded it. They therefore were not doing it or he would have felt no need to exhort them to do it. His first exhortation was in Philippians 3:1, 'Finally, my brothers, rejoice in the Lord!' It was repeated in Philippians 4:4: 'Rejoice in the Lord always. I will say it again: Rejoice!'

Paul inserts this second injunction in the context of a church quarrel that was going on in Philippi at the time:

> I plead with Euodia and I plead with Syntyche to agree with each other in the Lord. Yes, and I ask you, loyal yoke-fellow, help these women who have contended at my side in the cause of the gospel, along with Clement and the rest of my fellow-workers, whose names are in the book of life. (Philippians 4:2–3)

It is then that he adds, 'Rejoice in the Lord always. I will say it again: Rejoice!' Why ever would he put this to them then? Had he said, 'Lament' or 'Be sorry and repentant' it would have made sense. For he might have scolded them for allowing this squabble to take place; and we know how important unity was to Paul and its place in this epistle. Indeed, one could make the case that Philippi is as much about unity as joy. For early on he expresses hope that they will 'stand firm in one spirit, contending as one man for the faith of the gospel' (Phil. 1:27). He then said to them, '. . . make my joy complete by being like-minded, having the same love, being one in spirit and purpose' (Phil. 2:2). This became the context for the great Christological passage – Philippians 2:5–12.

Therefore when Paul addresses the division in the church at Philippi between the followers of Euodia and those of Syntyche – undoubtedly two powerful women, each of whom had their following and were accusing one another – we might expect a severe reprimand. But no. He says, 'Rejoice in the Lord'. Extraordinary!

But why? That is what this present chapter is about. I want to demonstrate the benefit of rejoicing, even when you certainly don't feel like rejoicing.

Let us look at Paul's plight. He had every reason at the time not to rejoice, humanly speaking. All the things that gave him the impetus to rejoice are the very things that would cast me down and keep me there! Consider that (1) he was in prison as he wrote, and (2) he was not being encouraged by fellow ministers at the time.

Rejoicing while he was in prison was something Paul perhaps learned, along with his friend Silas, when he was right there in Philippi a few years before. Paul and Silas were put in prison for preaching the gospel. However, instead of giving in to self-pity and raising the question, 'How could God let this happen to me?', they prayed and sang hymns to God (Acts 16:25)! Paul could not have known at that moment that he would one day be writing a letter to the believers at Philippi – from another prison, this time in Rome.

While he was in prison in Rome, then, he wrote to the Philippians. His opposition as he wrote this remarkable letter was not only from the world, but also from those in the church there who added to Paul's uneasy situation. He tells us himself what was going on:

> . . . it has become clear throughout the whole palace guard and to everyone else that I am in chains for Christ . . . some preach Christ out of envy and rivalry . . . out of selfish ambition, not sincerely, supposing that they can stir up trouble for me while I am in chains. (Philippians 1:13–17)

And what do you suppose was Paul's reaction to these people? It is quite amazing:

> But what does it matter? The important thing is that in every way, whether from false motives or true, Christ is preached. And because of this I rejoice. Yes, and I will continue to rejoice . . . (Philippians 1:18)

There are basically two kinds of rejoicing: (1) spontaneous rejoicing that comes quite involuntarily and from the overflow of good things happening around you – when you feel, and are, quite simply, happy; (2) rejoicing that comes from effort because it is not what you feel like doing. It is what you do because you know it is right. That is what Paul was doing here and that is the kind of rejoicing we are focusing on in this chapter.

It is what the ancient prophet Habakkuk chose to do, and it is one of the major triumphs of faith in the Old Testament. Hebrews 11, the great 'faith chapter' of the Bible, describes many stalwarts of faith who lived in Old Testament times. But obviously a lot of good examples were left out and the proof of that is this man Habakkuk. The writer of Hebrews did in fact quote from Habakkuk (Heb. 10:38; cf. Hab. 2:4) – 'my righteous one will live by faith' but in Hebrew reads, 'the righteous shall live by His faithfulness'. In other words, Habakkuk's faith was based on the fact that he lived by God's faithfulness; he believed that God was faithful. Habakkuk began his little book by dealing with the most difficult question there is: why does God allow evil and why do the righteous suffer?

Why do you make me look at injustice? Why do you tolerate wrong? (Habakkuk 1:3)

God's answer to Habakkuk's question was 'Wait':

For the revelation awaits an appointed time; it speaks of the end and will not prove false. Though it linger, wait for it; it will certainly come and will not delay. (Habakkuk 2:3)

This passage was the context for the writer of Hebrews in trying to encourage discouraged Jewish Christians. He urged them not to give up. Why? Because God – who is never too late, never too early, but always just on time – will step in to their situation:

So do not throw away your confidence; it will be richly rewarded. You need to persevere so that when you have done the will of God, you will receive what he has promised. For in just a very little while, 'He who is coming will come and will not delay. But my righteous one will live by faith'. (Hebrews 10:35–8)

It was a robust faith in the faithfulness of God to step in that kept Habakkuk himself going, and it is what the writer of Hebrews hopes will keep these Jewish Christians going. It is what should keep us all going – God is faithful.

But what do you suppose happened to Habakkuk himself? Did he get his question answered? Did he get the breakthrough he wanted? No. He got a different kind of breakthrough:'I will rejoice in the Lord'. Amazing! He didn't get what he wanted, but he is still rejoicing:

Though the fig-tree does not bud and there are no grapes on the vines, though the olive crop fails and the fields produce no food, though there are no sheep in the pen and no cattle in the stalls, *yet I will rejoice in the LORD, I will be joyful in God my Saviour.* (Habakkuk 3:17, my italics)

What Habakkuk was saying was this: if things don't get better, I will rejoice anyway. If I don't get my theological-philosophical questions answered (why does God allow evil and suffering to flourish?), I will still rejoice. If my prayers are not answered, I will rejoice. If I am not healed, I will rejoice. If I do not prosper as I wish to, I will rejoice. If I am by-passed for that honour or invitation I hoped for, I will rejoice. If the revival I prayed earnestly for is delayed, I will rejoice. If success comes to others, but not to me, I will rejoice. If I remain unvindicated, I will rejoice.

If Habakkuk could do this, so can I. If Paul could, I can.

Rejoicing is, more often than not, a choice. We all love spontaneous rejoicing. Such comes from answered prayer, the answers to our questions, the manifestation of the miraculous, the success and prosperity we wanted. It takes little faith to rejoice when it is precipitated by happy, external circumstances. But the command to rejoice comes because we don't always feel like rejoicing – and yet Paul said to do it all the time. Not rejoicing *because* of all that has happened but rather '*in* all circumstances' (1 Thessalonians 5:18). The choice we make to rejoice comes because we simply don't feel like rejoicing. *We have to just do it.*

There were apparently two kinds of rejoicing in the Old Testament era: (1) because the Law required it; and (2) out of gratitude. The first time the word 'rejoice' appears in the Bible is in Leviticus 23:40: 'On the first day you are to take choice fruit from the trees, and palm fronds, leafy branches and poplars, and rejoice before the LORD your God for seven days.' This was a requirement – what they had to do under the Law whether they felt like it or not; and this kind of injunction appeared frequently under the Law (Deut. 12:7, 12, 18, etc.).

But the choice to rejoice in the Old Testament era also came out of sheer gratitude and not from a legalistic motive. 'I will be glad and rejoice in you' (Ps. 9:2). In a psalm that indicates the hiding of God's face came also the words: 'But I trust in your unfailing love; my heart rejoices in your salvation' (Ps. 13:5). 'I will rejoice in your promise like one who finds great spoil' (Ps. 119:162). '. . . let the hearts of those who seek the LORD rejoice' (1 Chr. 16:10). These are not words that come from the overflow of happy circumstances; neither do they indicate that they are motivated by fear of punishment (which is the way the Law produced obedience), but out of a godly sense of thanks to God. This shows how you and I can live if we put our minds to it.

Some of us have ridiculed the popular idea of 'the power of positive thinking', mainly because of the lack of solid orthodoxy that tended to lie behind it. But there is something worthwhile in this that people like me could learn from. Negative thinking not only requires little or no grace; it plays abundantly into the devil's scheme for us. Rejoicing, thinking positively, usually requires great effort and is often a sign of great grace in our lives. It is exactly what we are told to do!

Jesus told us to rejoice in adverse conditions. The climax of the Beatitudes is a command to rejoice under the worst of circumstances. The best translation of *makarios* (usually translated 'blessed') is really 'congratulations'. Jesus thus says 'Congratulations' when people insult us or persecute us. 'Rejoice and be glad' (Matt. 5:11–12).

Jesus also commanded us to rejoice because our names are written in heaven. He implicitly rebuked his disciples because they were so excited over demons being subject to them. There are Christians, I fear, who put a higher priority over the miraculous, the signs, wonders and gifts of the Spirit, and forget the main thing: our names being written in heaven (Luke 10:20). Believe me, *that* is something to rejoice about! We should rejoice every day of the year that one day we are going to be in heaven. Life at its longest is still short, especially when compared to eternity (which has no end). I thank God I am not going to hell, but to heaven. Whatever is going wrong at this moment — whatever it is — the one thing that nobody can take from you and me is our citizenship in heaven (Phil. 3:20). I will never forget as long as I live the opening words of a prayer offered by Dr W.M. Tidwell when he visited Trevecca Nazarene College years ago: 'Lord, we thank you that we are not in hell.' Not many believe in hell today, but one day they will.

How do you rejoice when you don't feel like it? The answer is, you find things for which you certainly should be thankful and then discipline yourself to *voice that gratitude*. In one of my previous books, *Thanking God*, I tell how I go through my journal every morning, item by item of the previous day, and thank the Lord in detail for everything. I have been doing it for over fifteen years. My wife Louise and I frequently do this together. Recently, when returning to Key Largo in Florida (where we now live) from the airport, Louise said, 'Let's thank the Lord for twenty-five things that took place over the weekend.' We had a wonderful weekend in Connecticut. We began, taking turns, naming particular things — such as seeing the colour of the leaves at the height of the autumn in New England; standing on the spot where Jonathan Edwards preached his historic sermon 'Sinners in the hands of an angry God' (an event that has affected me profoundly); the good meeting at Groton; the lovely pastor and his wife — Jim and Louise Schnider; the sweet time with John Paul Jackson and his wife Diane in New Hampshire; how we enjoyed noting the English names of cities and towns wherever we went (did you know there is an Acton in Massachusetts?); the way our ministry was received – and many other little things in between. When we finished, Louise said we had mentioned fifty-three things. I think God liked that. It is the sort of thing you can make yourself do whether you feel like it or not. There are *always* things you can thank God for if you look around. In a word: if you don't feel like it, do it anyway,

On Christmas Eve 2002 our local newspaper, *The Miami Herald*, had an article on the front page with the headlines: 'Grateful attitude can make all the difference'. The article was based on a study carried out at the University of Miami. A scientific study based on 2,000 people over three years found that 'the most grateful people tend to be the happiest'. Dr Michael McCullough, professor of psychology, said that 'with gratitude, there is virtually no downside' and that there is a 'major upside: most grateful people have low rates of depression and negative moods – but high self-esteem'. Dr McCullough said that people can learn to be grateful. One study he worked on asked respondents to make daily notes on four or five things for which they were thankful – even if it was just a sunny day. The results: 'In just two to three weeks they reported being happier' and that 'people close to them could see the difference too'. Another psychologist, Dr Andrew Wenger, also involved in the project, which was called the Research Project on Gratitude and Thankfulness, concluded that 'grateful people are more likely to be resilient, and they seem to have an easier time overcoming obstacles'. I can only conclude that if a project like this, carried out on a secular basis, reached such conclusions, how much more ought we who are believers be determined to *voice gratitude* every day to our heavenly Father!

There is nothing better for overcoming depression or turning a negative mood away than thanking God for things and, simply, praising the Lord. If I may refer to my book *Thanking God* one more time, I mention there how I became convicted over the lack of emphasis on worship during my era at Westminster Chapel. Happily this changed at the Chapel, but also in my own private devotional life. Louise and I try to sing together for fifteen minutes every morning and I sing for ten minutes nearly each evening before retiring to bed. Sometimes the hymns or choruses that we sing have a way of speaking to us as to where we are in our pilgrimage and perspective, and that is of course quite wonderful. But there are other times I have wanted to choose hymns that do nothing other than proclaim the goodness of the Lord without any reference, if possible, to my present situation. Hymns like 'I'll praise my Maker while I've breath' or 'And can it be that I should gain an interest in my Saviour's blood?' or 'O worship the King'. Why? Because there is a place for doing nothing but *praising the Lord* without any reference to myself or present need. The funny thing is, believe it or not, doing this often has the effect of blessing you more than ever! In other words, you don't do it because you feel like it; you do it because it is right to do it. But the good feeling often follows the sheer discipline of showing thankfulness and praise to God.

Pewter said that we 'greatly rejoice' because of the resurrection of Jesus Christ from the dead and the hope of an inheritance that can never perish, spoil or fade, even though we may have to suffer grief in all kinds of trials (1 Pet. 1:4–6). Not only that; if we are in a painful trial we should 'rejoice' that we are participating 'in the sufferings of Christ' (1 Pet. 4:13). There can be no grander or greater privilege than this. But Peter learned this the hard way. In what could have been his finest hour – had he boldly stood up for the Lord while Jesus was taken into custody at the house of the high priest – Peter blew it instead. He was immediately found out, as Jesus predicted, by the crowing of a rooster. Peter sobbed his heart out in bitter shame (Luke 22:54–62). He could never get that moment back. That moment would stay with him as long as he lived.

However, Peter was given a second chance. Our God is the God of the 'second look', as the hymn writer John Newton put it. A few weeks later Peter stood in what may well have been the very spot where he denied the Lord Jesus. This time he himself was on trial for preaching that Jesus had been raised from the dead. After being flogged, the authorities severely warned him not to teach in Jesus's name. Instead of feeling humiliated (which was intended to be part of his punishment), the opposite was the case! Lo and behold, he and John left 'rejoicing because they had been *counted worthy of suffering disgrace* for the Name' (Acts 5:41, my italics). God gave Peter a second chance and he grasped it with both hands. Suffering shame is not what most of us want to experience, but it became the most wonderful moment of Peter's life after having let the Lord down a few weeks before. This is why he said later on:

Dear friends, do not be surprised at the painful trial you are suffering, as though something strange were happening to you. But rejoice that you participate in the sufferings of Christ, so that you may be overjoyed when his glory is revealed. If you are insulted because of the name of Christ, you are blessed, for the Spirit of glory and of God rests on you. (1 Peter 4:12–14)

Do you feel that you let God down sometimes? Haven't we all? God will come again, one way or another, to let us have another chance – and (perhaps) save face! Rejoice in his faithfulness. Rejoice in the way he covers for us, and does not expose the skeletons in our cupboards. God is so kind and gracious.

When Paul told the Philippians to rejoice in the Lord in the context of a church quarrel, he didn't mean for them to be happy about the situation between Syntyche and Euodia. In the same way, he is not asking us to be excited about the bad things that may have happened in our lives or in the world around us, but he is trying to get our minds on something useful and positive because – one day – we will be glad we did. Whatever you are going through, this too will work together for good (Rom. 8:28).

The rejoicing that Peter experienced after being rebuked and flogged by the ruling council in Jerusalem showed how much he had changed. He was cowardly after Jesus was arrested, but now he was as bold as a lion. God wants to do this for all of us. He lets us have a second chance after we have blown it. This alone is cause for rejoicing.

There is a word that is closely akin to 'rejoice', and that is to 'delight' (Greek *eudokeo*). Paul used it in 2 Corinthians 12:10: '. . . I delight in weaknesses, in insults, in hardships, in persecutions, in difficulties'. He said this because of the 'thorn in the flesh' God had allowed in him to keep him 'from being conceited'. (I deal with this in detail in my book called *Thorn in the Flesh*.) Paul had prayed for God to take it away, but was told instead by the Lord, 'My grace is sufficient for you, for my power is made perfect in weakness' (2 Cor. 12:9). This is when Paul used *eudokeo*: 'That is why, for Christ's sake, I delight in weaknesses . . . For when I am weak, then I am strong' (2 Cor. 12:10). *Eudokeo* means 'to take pleasure in', but strongly implies volition. In other words, Paul made a choice to delight in what was painful because it gave the Lord a greater opportunity to display his power in Paul without Paul getting the glory. I myself was comforted by this insight when I found it in one of my books on Greek. I refer to a Greek word if I think it will be helpful for the reader or listener. In this case, it certainly helped me! This is because I used to feel guilty that I did not naturally delight in weaknesses, insults, etc. I used to pray that God would make me spiritual enough to delight when adverse things happened; but when I learned that it is a word that implies volition, I was set free to realise that Paul did not *naturally* rejoice, but rather *chose* to delight in these things. I can live with that! I can choose to rejoice, but I cannot help it if I do not feel like it at first. As for a thorn in the flesh – which almost all of us have to some extent – it is very, very painful. It is an acute form of chastening. Paul chose to delight in it because of its benefit to himself and the kingdom of God.

But there is one further important clarification: we are told to *rejoice in the Lord*. We do not rejoice in ourselves, or things. We rejoice in the Lord Jesus. This we can always do because there is no fault in him, no disappointment. We rejoice in his person – that he is totally God and totally man. He was and is God as though he were not man, and man as though he were not God. There is a man in glory as you read these lines. He is there in heaven at God's right hand, doing basically two things: (1) reigning over all creation (1 Cor. 15:25), and (2) interceding for the elect, referred to in Hebrews 7:25 as those who come to God through him. No matter what our circumstances we can always – with integrity – rejoice in the Lord Jesus Christ. We rejoice that we have been forgiven (Eph. 1:7), that we have been set free from the Law (Gal. 5:1), and that we are destined for heaven because nothing can stop that. We can always rejoice, as I have said above, that we are going to heaven and not to hell. Even at our lowest point we should always be able to rejoice *in the Lord*.

The same Lord we rejoice in, however, is not only in heaven. He is with us wherever we are. Paul said that he was at hand (Phil. 4:5); Paul could thus speak of Jesus being right there with him: '. . . the Lord stood at my side and gave me strength' (2 Tim. 4:17). How could this be if he is in heaven? Is it because he miraculously remains there and yet comes to us where we are? Certainly. But it is also because he lifts us up to where he is! 'God raised us up with Christ and seated us with him in the heavenly realms in Christ Jesus' (Eph. 2:6). After all, among Jesus's last words were: 'And surely I am with you always, to the very end of the age' (Matt. 28:20). 'Never will I leave you; never will I forsake you' (Heb. 13:5). In this place the writer uses a word that really means, 'I will never, never, never, never leave you nor forsake you'! That is therefore perpetual cause for rejoicing.

I love the psalm in which David says, 'God is for me' (Ps. 56:9). There is no greater feeling than to know that 'God is on my side' (Ps. 118:6, AV). 'If God is for us, who can be against us?' (Rom. 8:31). To know that God is with us and 'for' us is a great cause for rejoicing. This always makes me think of my Grandpa McCurley, who was almost the only relative who stood with me when my theological views changed in 1955–6. 'I'm for him, right or wrong,' he said to the rest of the family in those days. That was the kind of support I needed at that time. And yet that is how much God is with us and for us all the time!

This does not mean he approves of all we believe and do. Yes, he is for us – right or wrong; but it does not follow he will uphold my unrighteous cause. He is able to be for me – whether I deserve it or not – in order to demonstrate patience that I might be brought to repentance and get sorted out, if that is what needs to happen. The amazing thing is, he still maintains love and support for me when I am unworthy. He sees the end from the beginning. He does not have to defend his love for me to anybody. In the same way that Jesus did not defend his choice of disciples (some of whom raised the eyebrows of self-righteous people), so does he not have to explain himself for maintaining an everlasting love towards us, even when we are in the wrong. This is why we should not be self-righteous if we feel the presence of the Lord and claim this proves we are in the right. God has a way of manifesting his presence to the most unworthy child! That is why he can be real to me. It does not mean I am better than others or that God approves of all he sees in me. He is that way with all his children! He stays with them until they get sorted out. What love! Amazing love! This is why we rejoice – always . . . in the Lord.

5

The Immediate Witness
of the Holy Spirit

We are witnesses of these things, and so is the Holy Spirit,
whom God has given to those who obey him. (Acts 5:32)

During my time at Oxford I was pastor of a church in
Lower Heyford. While there I wrote a catechism that I based
on certain principles of the glory of God. I asked Dr Martyn
Lloyd-Jones to read it and give his opinion. He insisted on
one change: that the question and answer referring to assurance of salvation and the witness of the Holy Spirit should
refer to the *immediate and direct* witness of the Spirit, not just
witness of the Spirit. I felt I knew what he meant by that,
but it was the first time I realised how important this issue
was to him.

I was at Oxford to study the Puritans. In my thesis I

called them 'experimental predestinarians'. This is because by and large they emphasised two things: (1) predestination; and (2) assurance of salvation by good works. They used what they called a 'practical syllogism', based on Aristotelian reasoning:

1. all who are predestined to salvation will manifest sanctification (hypothesis);
2. but my life manifests sanctification (antithesis);
3. therefore I am predestined to salvation (conclusion).

In other words, they came to assurance of salvation by an experiment; if you were godly, you knew you were saved. How did you know you were godly? Because you keep the works of the Law.

Therefore if you were experiencing sanctification you could be sure you met the conditions of the practical syllogism: you are one of God's elect. This manner of coming to assurance was called by most of them 'the reflex act of faith' or 'indirect act of faith'. They used this kind of language because they did not directly trust the merit of Christ. There was no warrant for faith until there was undoubted sanctification. If you could reflect upon the evidence of sanctification you could conclude you were saved. Not directly, but indirectly. But you could none the less conclude that you were saved. With few exceptions, this was the standard position of the Puritans on the matter of assurance.

This way of thinking is *not* my own position. I highly respect those godly people called Puritans and I am indebted to them more than I can say. But in much the same way as we look at our parents' imperfections as we grow older and are emancipated from them, this is the way my relationship with the Puritans has been. I came to realise that the Puritans' doctrine of assurance, generally speaking, is inadequate – and I fear that it even leads to legalism and self-righteousness. There is a much better way to know that you are saved, as we will see.

However, one must grant the validity of the practical syllogism when it comes to the assurance of salvation. One can use the same reasoning without being vulnerable to legalism. For example:

1. all who trust the blood of Jesus, not their good works, will be saved;
2. but I trust wholly in the blood of Jesus for my salvation;
3. therefore I am saved.

This is using the practical syllogism in a manner that is edifying and comforting. The sad thing about the Puritans' way of coming to assurance was that it seldom worked. Both the leading Puritans themselves, as well as their hearers, struggled right up to their deaths with the question of whether or not they were truly saved. The reason: they were not sure they were sanctified *enough*. They always felt they must do a bit more, be more godly and more conscientious. Few met the standard.

In this chapter I want us to see that there are basically two levels of coming to true assurance of salvation: (1) the indirect act of faith; and (2) the direct witness of the Spirit. We will focus on the latter in this chapter, but it is helpful to understand more with regard to the first level or otherwise we may not appreciate the importance of the immediate witness of the Spirit.

The first level of assurance – the reflective or indirect act of faith – is the way most of us initially come to assurance of salvation. Take John 3:16, which Martin Luther called 'the Bible in a nutshell' – 'For God so loved the world that he gave his one and only Son, that whoever believes in him shall not perish but have eternal life.' I apply John 3:16 like this: I trust God's one and only Son; therefore I know I have eternal life. The Spirit applies the word as I apply the gospel to my own life. Therefore assurance is *mediated* by the Spirit. The Holy Spirit is at work, yes. He enables me to believe the gospel. I apply the promise – I believe it! I therefore know I am saved. It is not an immediate witness of the Spirit in this case, but true assurance none the less *mediated* by the Spirit as I apply the gospel.

I am a great believer in a soul-winning programme called Evangelism Explosion. It was designed by Dr D. James Kennedy, the minister of the Coral Ridge Presbyterian Church in Fort Lauderdale, Florida. There are two 'diagnostic questions' one asks someone – regardless of whether they are non-Christians or professing Christians (it does not matter): (1) 'Do you know for sure that if you were to die today you would go to heaven?' (2) 'If you stood before God and he were to ask you, "Why should I let you into my heaven?", what would you say?' In most cases, people we meet will say they think they would get into heaven – if there is such a place – by their good works. At this stage one presents the gospel. Should these people accept the gospel and pray the 'sinner's prayer', we then say to that person: 'Who have you just trusted for your salvation?' If they reply, 'Jesus who died for me on the cross,' we then say, 'That being true and if you died today, where would you go?' They would reply 'To heaven'. Many times the people will be tearful or emotional, sometimes not. In either case, the question is put in such a manner that they *reflect* on what they have just done (trusting Christ for their salvation). They are thus assured of being converted, born again. I am certainly not saying that all who pray the prayer or who give the right answers are absolutely saved. I am only pointing out that this is a way many of us have come to realise that we have the hope of heaven; it is because we know we have trusted Christ. It is the reflective act – the indirect act of faith. God uses this and it has considerable comfort and assurance to many.

In this chapter I want to show, however, that there is a higher level of assurance than that which I have just described, valid and sound though it is. Because it *is* sound, there are many who do not want to consider anything beyond this as a way of God being more real, having greater assurance, or an experience that is beyond conversion. Many are offended at the thought and even get defensive. Why should anybody be defensive over the possibility of having more of God and a greater measure of assurance? But sometimes they are, and they appeal to verses like 1 Corinthians 1:7 ('you do not lack any spiritual gift') or perhaps Ephesians 1:3 (we are blessed 'with every spiritual blessing in Christ') as a way of saying that you get everything God has for you in one package – conversion. This either fits one's chosen theological position or, sometimes but not always, it plays into the more worldly sort of Christian who doesn't want to get too spiritual. Whatever the reason, it is not necessary to be defensive, but instead excited, that God wants to do even more for us. It is not subsequent to salvation, but *included in* the blessing of being a part of the family of God.

Many good Christians have only a soteriological doctrine of the Spirit. Soteriology refers to salvation, so a soteriological doctrine of the Spirit is the Spirit *applying* the gospel. The Holy Spirit witnesses that I believe this gospel because my hope is in Christ's death alone. There is nothing wrong with having a doctrine of the Spirit that gives assurance through knowing you have believed the gospel. But, sadly, that is the limit of some people's understanding of the Spirit. They have no place in their understanding for the *immediate and direct* witness of the Spirit.

There is therefore a higher level of assurance than that mediated by faith in the word. It is the immediate and direct witness of the Spirit. This is pure joy. And yet this higher level of assurance does not make a person 'more' a Christian than they already were. This is because embracing the gospel is what saves you, and once you are saved you are as saved as you can get. The essence of faith is trusting the blood of Christ alone. You are either trusting Christ alone or you are not. If you are, you are saved. And if you are trusting Christ alone, you know that you are trusting him. But that is assurance by reflection – it is the indirect act of faith and not the direct witness of the Spirit, comforting though it is.

One could say that the knowledge of your sins being

forgiven, even by the reflective act of faith or soteriological application of the gospel, is pure joy. For it is. And if something is pure, it is pure! Therefore if I now call the immediate witness of the Spirit *pure joy* it would seem I am devaluing the joy that comes when someone first realises that their sins are totally forgiven and washed away by the blood of Jesus. This is the last thing I would want to do. But I would illustrate what I wish to describe like this. I will never forget my first view of the Swiss Alps. It came as our family drove from Germany into Switzerland many years ago. I was almost overwhelmed by the beauty. I had never seen anything like it. And yet I was not prepared for what was to be seen two hours later when we arrived at Inter-laken. The sight of the little village nestled between two lakes with the majestic Jungfrau and other snow-capped mountains in the background made our initial glimpse of Switzerland – by comparison – seem less dazzling. The truth is, all of Switzerland is beautiful, but it seemed that the further we drove and the higher we climbed, the more beautiful it became. That is the way knowing God is. It gets better and better.

The joy that comes from the immediate and direct witness of the Spirit, which gives the highest form of assurance, more often than not (for some reason) does not come at conversion. It usually comes later on – whether days later, months later, or years later. And yet it *can and sometimes does* come at conversion. I don't mean to make it complicated, but the truth is that Cornelius and those with him received the Holy Spirit in an immediate and direct manner when they were initially converted (see

Acts 10:44–6). This is proof that one may experience this at conversion. But I must also say that it would seem to be the exception to the rule, which both Scripture and experience will bear out. The immediate witness of the Spirit, speaking generally, comes subsequent to conversion. This was the experience of Saul of Tarsus. He was converted on the road to Damascus, but is said to be 'filled with the Spirit' later on when Ananias laid hands on him (Acts 1:1–19). In the case of certain believers in Samaria, they were converted because they 'accepted the word of God', but at the same time the Holy Spirit 'had not yet come upon any of them'. This awaited Peter and John who laid hands on them 'and they received the Holy Spirit' (Acts 8:15–17). This was true of Christians at Ephesus as well (Acts 19:1–6).

It ought to go without saying that the disciples of Jesus – with the exception of Judas Iscariot (John 17:12) – were converted men. They were saved before the day of Pentecost. But they were not *filled* with the Spirit until that day (Acts 2:4). This filling is called being baptised with the Holy Spirit because moments before his ascension to heaven Jesus said, '. . . in a few days you will be baptised with the Holy Spirit' (Acts 1:5). Both Scripture and the experiences of people throughout the history of the Christian Church tend to demonstrate that the baptism of the Spirit – or whatever you want to call it – comes after one's conversion to Christ.

And yet the baptism of the Spirit is not the only term to describe what we are here referring to as the immediate and direct witness of the Spirit. Jesus called it *rest for the soul* (Matt. 11:29) – the exact same thing. He equally meant this when he said that the Father wanted to give the Holy Spirit to those who ask him (Luke 11:13). Paul called it the sealing of the Spirit (Eph. 1:13; 2 Cor. 1:22). He also called it 'the good deposit' (2 Tim. 1:14) as well as 'renewal by the Holy Spirit' (Titus 3:5). The writer of Hebrews called it 'God's rest' (Heb. 4:1, 10); God swearing an oath to us like he did to Abraham (Heb. 6:13–20), and receiving the promise (Heb. 10:35–7). John referred to it as perfect love which casts out fear and gives boldness in the day of judgement (1 John 4:17–18).

What I am attempting to describe in this chapter came to me several years after my conversion. I was converted at the age of six on 5 April 1942, but on 31 October 1955, driving in my car from my little church in Palmer, Tennessee (my first pastorate), on my way to Trevecca Nazarene College in Nashville (where I was a student), the most extraordinary joy and peace came to my heart. I did not know anything like that was possible here on this planet. I was utterly and totally surprised. I wasn't even aware of seeking such an experience; I am sure I would have done had I known it existed. But I didn't know it; I was just spending the time in prayer because I felt desperate for more of God. I cried out to the Lord in agony. Lo and behold, the glory of the Lord filled the car. I was taken up into the heavenlies – and yet I continued to drive. There was Jesus interceding for me with all his heart at the right hand of the Father. I burst into tears. I saw that the Lord cared more for me than I did myself. An hour later – how I drove I will not know until I get to heaven and ask for a video replay – I entered into a *rest of soul* that led not only to a change of heart, but of theology!

And I am not even coming close to describing what it was like.

We are therefore talking about inner joy. It is not a happiness that comes from outside things – like a pay rise, a new job, vindication, a letter with good news, or receiving a coveted invitation. It is within. It does not come from a practical syllogism, reflecting on my reliance on Christ, or any reasoning at all. It is greater than reasoning, and actually by-passes reasoning. You don't need to reason it out or deduce this or that or draw a conclusion by logical deduction. It is immediate and direct. It is the Holy Spirit himself. It is not the Spirit applying the word; it is the Spirit's own witness. It is he himself taking his abode. No word can adequately explain it. When Rodney Howard-Browne was criticised for saying some people need a 'head by-pass operation' I knew what he meant! This baptism comes straight to the heart. Our heads, our brains and our biases get in the way.

It is the Spirit's *own* witness. It is indeed the person of the Holy Spirit himself coming right inside of you. This is why it is called immediate and direct. With syllogistic reasoning the Holy Spirit applies the word; we use our minds to apply what we have heard and are thus able safely to conclude that we are going to heaven. But our minds applied the word and *then* it touched the heart. But this *rest of soul* – the result of the immediate and direct witness of the Spirit – comes without any reasoning, applying, thinking, deducting or reflecting. It is the Spirit overruling our minds and going directly to the heart – straight from heaven to the soul. It is an act of God, sovereignly bestowed, and there is not one thing you can do to *make* it happen. And yet Jesus tells us it is what the Father delights to do for those who ask him.

One further fruit of this is how the Bible comes alive – you know more than ever that the Bible is the very word of God. John Calvin taught that we know the Bible is the word of God by the 'inner testimony of the Spirit'. I am not suggesting that Calvin was teaching the same thing as in this chapter. I do not believe one needs the baptism of the Spirit to believe that the Bible is the word of God, but I am certainly saying that it enables you to believe it more than ever! All of it! You know you have not been deceived. You see clearly and without doubt that Christianity is true, the Christian faith is real, and that Jesus is real. His resurrection is real.

This is what Acts 4:33 conveys. The translations vary, though. The New International Version says, 'With great power the apostles continued to testify to the resurrection of the Lord Jesus, and much grace was upon them all.' The Authorised Version says, 'And with great power gave the apostles witness of the resurrection of the Lord Jesus.' The Greek literally says 'the apostles were given great power of the witness of the resurrection of the Lord Jesus'. I do not doubt that they did *preach* this and did so with power, but that is not what the Greek literally says. It only says that the apostles were given great power of the *witness* of the resurrection. I have long understood this verse as referring to what they *felt,* not how they preached. Most translations, in my opinion, unwittingly gloss over the real point Luke was trying to make. His point here was that, after their unusual prayer meeting where the *place* was shaken (Acts 4:31), there was a fresh falling of the Spirit – immediately and directly into their hearts – that enabled them to *feel* the resurrection with great power. The resurrection of Jesus was so real to them at that time that their being present at the very tomb of Jesus on Easter morning – and seeing him raised – would not have been any more convincing. Talk about joy! It is knowing you've got it right, not because of how much you have read or how much teaching you have received, but by the presence of the Holy Spirit in power. Nothing at all compares with this.

This also indicates that the immediate witness of the Holy Spirit can (1) happen more than once, and (2) refer to more than an assurance that you are saved. On the first point, one must never forget that when the power of God fell to the extent that the very place – the building – was shaken (as if by a small earthquake) and the apostles experienced this power, it was like a *renewed baptism of the Spirit*. In other words, what happened in Acts 2:4 happened again in Acts 4:31ff.

This is so encouraging. Whereas conversion can only take place once – which is why there is only one baptism (Ephesians 4:4) – the filling of the Spirit need not be a once-for-all experience. Indeed, Paul's injunction that we be filled with the Spirit (Eph. 5:18) means that it *should* keep happening.

The second point, that the immediate witness of the Spirit need not only refer to assurance of salvation, indicates that such presence of the Spirit may relate to many things. Its initial occurrence almost certainly would relate to one's full assurance of salvation. But the renewal of the immediate witness of the Spirit may refer to guidance and doctrine, answers to prayers in advance, discernment, and other pertinent matters in the kingdom of God.

There are therefore varied levels of the immediate witness of the Spirit. There are degrees of intensity from one individual to another and also different ways that the Spirit relates to a particular person. For example, what happened to me may not have happened to you, and what may have been your experience may not have been mine. In my case, I did not speak in tongues. That came later. This to me shows that it is wrong to say that speaking in tongues is the necessary evidence of the baptism of the Spirit. I think the essential and necessary evidence of the filling of the Spirit is joy. Pure joy.

In my own experience I was given an understanding of theology that possibly does not come to some. I cannot explain the reason for this unless it is because I have had a keen interest in theology that goes back to my teenage years. You therefore may receive this immediate witness of the Spirit in a manner that coheres with the way God made you and shaped you, and it may be different from another's experience. I was given witness of the resurrection of Jesus, and this is why I have interpreted Acts 4:33 as I do above. The resurrection of Jesus was so real to me for days and days after 31 October 1955 that I felt I could say with transparent integrity that I know for a fact Jesus was raised from the dead!

Perhaps the most important result to me was my understanding of salvation. I was simply given an understanding of grace – sovereign grace – that went right across much I had been taught as a child. Why? You tell me. I only know that within hours of entering into this rest of faith I knew I was eternally saved (and could never be lost) and that the work of the Spirit is sovereign in people. You could call it predestination. Believe me, I came to embrace things that my old church not only did not teach, but taught against! And yet I have never looked back and I thank God for graciously showing me reformed theology. It was revelation by the Spirit. I did not get it from anybody teaching me or from reading a book. It was immediate and direct by the Holy Spirit and – at one time – I thought I was the first to experience this since the apostle Paul!

I will share with you something amusing. Call it an irony if you like. Because of my change of theology I found my way into ranks of people who applauded my discovery – except for one thing. They tended to be 'cessationists' – the view that the miraculous *ceased* after the days of the early Church. The view of cessationists is that we do not need the miraculous today – we have the Bible. They claim that once the canon of Scripture was complete, God withdrew the miraculous from the Church and wanted us to grow up and know his word and lean entirely upon it. We are mature people now, they said, and don't need signs, wonders, miracles. (This would include experiences of the Spirit like my own.) The cessationists affirmed my theology, but denied the experience that led me straight to it!

I used to say to them, 'If my experience led me to Jehovah's Witness teaching or that of some cult, you would have to say that what happened to me was of the devil. But what happened to me brought me right into the heart of reformed theology. I never read a book on it, so it could not have come from inside me. How do you explain that my experience could not have been of God merely because God does not do that sort of thing today?' They did not want to talk about it. My friend Jack Taylor puts it like this: many people's doctrine of the Trinity is 'God the Father, God the Son and God the Holy Bible'. My Calvinist friends would say, 'What you say happened to you can't happen today.' I would reply, 'But it did.' I should point out, though, that many reformed people today are *not* cessationists, although some of them are.

In any case, the undoubted evidence of the filling of the Holy Spirit is not sound theology – or speaking in tongues. As for one being filled with the Spirit and not being theologically sophisticated, I have to say that it is not only possible, but is often the case! Because my own experience led me to what I regard as sound theology, I used to think that the proof that one is Spirit-filled would be that he or she too would affirm election, predestination, effectual calling and the security of the believer (once saved, always saved). But I was wrong to expect this of everybody. I had to climb down and admit that God *did* baptise many, many people with the Spirit *without* changing their theology. John Wesley is a good example of this. The true sign of the immediate witness of the Spirit is pure joy – from within.

We have noted above some references to the conveying of the Spirit through the laying on of hands. The apostles apparently had this power. Timothy's anointing came that way (1 Tim. 4:14). The writer of Hebrews even referred to the laying on of hands as a doctrine, indeed one of six principles that he called *elementary*, which went along-side such teachings as repentance, faith, resurrection and eternal judgement (Heb. 6:1–2). It sometimes referred to apostolic approval; that is, if you laid hands on someone – as in ordination – you must know that person and be prepared to recommend them (1 Tim. 5:22). Joshua was blessed by having the laying on of hands by Moses, but that occasion signalled more than mere approval. Indeed, 'Now Joshua son of Nun was filled with the spirit of wisdom *because* Moses had laid his hands on him' (Deut. 34:9, my italics). In other words, Joshua's high level of anointing was attributed to the laying on of hands by Moses. It meant more than just approval.

The teaching of laying on of hands is fascinating but also mysterious. I don't claim to understand it. We are not given to know all we would like to know about it, but there is obviously often an anointing that is not transferred in any other way. This means that, in God's plan and strategy, he has set the laying on of hands in motion for his glory – perhaps to confound the sophisticated. For one thing, it was once an exclusive apostolic privilege, but that is not the case today. Ordinary, non-clergy and untrained people of all ages seem to have the gift – at least at times – of the laying on of hands. Sometimes a child can administer the laying on of hands, and the result can be anything from deliverance to speaking in tongues or even holy laughter.

Back in the spring of 1994 when my friend Charlie Colchester first told Lyndon Bowring and me about the strange phenomenon of falling down and laughter that had broken out in his church – Holy Trinity Brompton – two weeks before, I did not believe it was of God. He told of one lady, who was visiting Britain from Grand Rapids, Michigan, with a reformed background, who began laying her hands on people and – to her amazement – they fell down and roared with laughter. Some readers will recognise this as the 'Toronto Blessing', as it was termed by the *Sunday Telegraph* and others. It passed from person to person through the laying on of hands. People began going to particular churches where it broke out, like Holy Trinity Brompton, Queens Road Baptist in Wimbledon, or flying all the way to Toronto where it started. The question was often raised, understandably, why do you have to go to a particular church to receive this blessing? Could you not be prayed for at a distance? Cannot God grant this blessing by remote control?

Of course he can, but sometimes God tests our earnestness to see if we will be humble enough to seek him to the extent that we will go anywhere it takes – and do anything – for more of him. That is what God required of Naaman, the commander of the army of the king of Aram, but also a leper. He was told first to seek Elisha the prophet, which meant going over into Israel. And then Elisha refused to see him! But Elisha did give instructions that greatly annoyed the proud general: 'Go, wash yourself seven times in the Jordan, and your flesh will be restored and you will be cleansed' (2 Kgs. 5:10). Naaman's reply was, 'Are not Abana and Pharpar, the rivers of Damascus, better than any of the waters of Israel?' This is like those who say, 'I can pray wherever I please, even at home without going to church at all.' True. But sometimes God places his anointing in a church that is not my own and I must have the meekness to admit this. Why Toronto, Holy Trinity Brompton or Queens Road, and not my church? You tell me. I only know that in the case of Naaman, he was not healed until he had the humility to do what Elisha commanded. In my case, I had to ascend my pulpit at Westminster Chapel and climb down! I said I was wrong to criticise what was happening in these churches. I publicly affirmed what was happening at Holy Trinity and prayed that morning for Sandy Millar and the people there. I have never been sorry that I did this, I can tell you that! But it was humbling, I can tell you that as well.

God loves to offend the sophisticated. There are two scriptures I sometimes quote when people ask for biblical support for things such as the Toronto Blessing:

But God chose the foolish things of the world to shame the wise; God chose the weak things of the world to shame the strong. He chose the lowly things of this world and the despised things – and the things that are not – to nullify the things that are, so that no-one may boast before him. (1 Corinthians 1:27–9)

'For my thoughts are not your thoughts, neither are your ways my ways,' declares the LORD. 'As the heavens are higher than the earth, so are my ways higher than your ways and my thoughts than your thoughts'. (Isaiah 55:8–9)

Paul Cain often says that God offends the mind to reveal the heart. I do not know many things that are more offensive than being prayed for, losing the ability to stand – and to fall down. I also think God looks high and low over the earth to find what will be obnoxious to smug and satisfied people. When he came up with people falling down and displaying emotions in front of everyone, I think maybe God said, 'That will do nicely'. If our hearts are not pliable and right with him, he can send things that annoy us to expose our pride and recalcitrance. Everything Jesus did seemed to offend the religious people of his day. The Holy Spirit continues the work of Jesus and upholds the exact same thing!

The most over-the-top demonstration of all was when God decreed that people will go to heaven only and solely because his Son died on a cross and shed his precious blood that those who believe in him will not perish but have eternal life. You would never have convinced the rabbis, the Pharisees, the Scribes, the Sadducees – *anybody* – that what was happening outside the city of Jerusalem on Good Friday was entirely God's idea and nobody else's. He has been doing the same ever since.

One of the things that convinced me that the Toronto Blessing was of God was the way people described the peace they felt inside. The joy of laughter was outward, but it happened because of what they were feeling in their hearts. I wish I could say as I write these lines that this laughter has happened to me. But it hasn't – yet. It has happened to my wife and some of my closest friends. Indeed, the ministry of Rodney Howard-Browne has done more to change Louise's life than nearly anything else I can think of.

Rodney Howard-Browne is apparently one of the chief

instruments God used in the phenomenon of 'holy laughter'. His ministry of laying on hands to Randy Clark – the man who passed it on to the Airport Christian Fellowship in Toronto – has led to this phenomenon of laughter all over the globe. The definitive treatment of how deep and how far the Toronto Blessing has impacted the world and individuals over a period of time has not been written yet (to my knowledge). John Arnott, the pastor of the Airport Christian Fellowship in Toronto, has shared with me some reports done by sociologists who approached the matter with objectivity and interviewed hundreds of people who claimed to be blessed by this ministry. I know that John was very encouraged over the findings. Some (most likely because they were not happy about it) dismissed the Toronto Blessing as a passing fad, or religious sideshow, that will soon be forgotten. I predict that this will not be the case. I get more reports all the time from countries in remotest places that continue to be impacted, including Third World nations. People still make pilgrimages to Toronto and find unusual power there, different to that which they witness in most other places. I regard this phenomenon as the embryonic phase of what may well turn out to be the greatest work of the Spirit since the days of the early Church.

Before I became the minister of Westminster Chapel in 1977 I preached at my little church in Lower Heyford that the revival for which many have been praying is *not* the charismatic movement. I repeated this at the first Word and Spirit Conference with Paul Cain at the Wembley Conference Centre in 1992. It was my view nearly thirty years ago, and is still my view today, that what we can expect is like Isaac being born after Ishmael. For thirteen years Ishmael was perceived by his father Abraham as the promised child he had been waiting for. Many today (for all I know) still suppose that the charismatic movement is *it*. Wrong. God said to Abraham in so many words, 'Ishmael is not the promised child you were expecting. Your wife Sarah will conceive. Isaac is coming' (see Gen. 17:15–22). Sarah gave birth to Isaac, and Isaac means 'laughter'. It is my view that God has been pleased to begin a great work of the Spirit in the Church throughout the world and it is often accompanied by the seemingly foolish phenomenon of laughter. Isaac will be an 'ugly baby', said Paul Cain a year before the Toronto Blessing broke out and spread like wild fire all over the world. 'But as an ugly baby often turns out to be a most beautiful child, so this baby will prove to be the most handsome child you can imagine.'

The laughter is not foolish; it is very holy and sacred. I have watched it up close. I have talked to those who have experienced it. I have seen it change lives (for the good). I have seen depression go, anointing increase, a love for God and the Bible follow, and a desire to worship and honour him – like nothing that ever came along that I know of. Often when I have talked with people who have experienced this I have been envious. I have known the peace and the joy, but not the laughter. I can only conclude that those who have experienced this laughter have had even greater joy than I have had, although I cannot prove that. Or perhaps this laughter came to those who were hurt the most. My wife Louise, for example, had been in a very severe depression for years. It was horrible for her and for me too. God knew exactly what to do for her: she was touched by this laughter through Rodney's ministry in early 1995 and she has not been the same since. She was not only healed, but given a fervour and devotion to the Lord that I can only describe as very extraordinary. I ought to know.

In a word: this joy and laughter is the result of the immediate and direct witness of the Spirit, and yet it sometimes causes those who engage in this laughter to feel utterly carefree and even to lose a sense of dignity. I have observed those who by nature are the most 'prim and proper' to laugh their heads off and not to care (at the time) what people think.

Recently, three drunken women got in a lift with me at a hotel where I was addressing a conference. They were laughing with each other uproariously – not caring in the slightest what anybody else in the lift was thinking. One fell on the floor of the lift as it ascended. The three laughed all the more. You may think I am getting ready to say they were a part of the conference I had been preaching to, but they had come from the bar of the hotel. They were simply drunk. I wondered at first if they had been at the conference, because I have seen the exact same thing when people have been sober as far as alcohol is concerned, but filled with the Spirit and behaving like drunks. At one of Rodney's meetings two people had to carry Louise to the lift and walk her to her room, then help her open the door to get in. This has made me wonder if this was not what was going on among the 120 at Pentecost. Surely there is nothing about speaking in tongues that would cause people to mock, 'They have had too much wine' (Acts 2:13)? There must have been more than speaking in other languages going on. I truly believe it was this laughter. Pure joy. This surely was why Paul compared wine to being filled with the Spirit when he said, 'Do not get drunk on wine, which leads to debauchery. Instead, be filled with the Spirit' (Eph. 5:18).

The immediate witness of the Spirit is described by Jesus in John 7:38: 'Whoever believes in me, as the Scripture has said, streams of living water will flow from within him.' The words 'from within', which the Authorised Version translates as 'out of his belly', come from *koilia*, a word that means the 'hollow of the body', 'stomach' or 'intestines'. The Hebraic mind conceived of worship as flowing from the entire body of a person. We all feel at times with our 'gut'. The seat of fear is that sinking feeling in the pit of the stomach. But it is also the seat of the feeling of joy. It comes deep from within. I have watched some people laugh, when the laughter was coming from the pit of the stomach, with such hilarity that it made me weep with joy. It often is so healing. Our son T.R. was with Louise at one of Rodney's meetings; T.R. looked at his watch and noted that she laughed incessantly for forty-five minutes. I know one thing: she returned home a transformed woman.

I stated above that my speaking in tongues came some time after my baptism in the Spirit. It was in fact approximately five months later and I was driving my car on this occasion too. I was not prepared for this, nor was I seeking for any gift. All I know is, I felt a sense of God – deep inside. It was like a well inside me that wanted to erupt. It was what Jesus described in John 7:38, only this time I felt a stirring inside that wanted to come out of my mouth, and then out came unintelligible sounds. It lasted only a second or two. Other supernatural phenomena occurred then also which I will not go into. The point is, this was an occasion of the immediate and direct work of the Spirit – indeed, the Holy Spirit himself in me to manifest the glory of the Lord. The feeling that day was an indescribable joy. To try to describe the peace and presence of the Holy Spirit in words, especially to one who has not yet experienced it, is like trying to describe a place of beauty to one who has not been there.

God wants all his children to experience pure joy, but I am not saying that all must have exactly the same manifestations. As I said, I have never fallen to the floor in laughter. You may or may not speak in tongues (see 1 Cor. 12:30). The necessary evidence of the baptism or sealing of the Spirit is this peace and joy. If, however, you say, 'The one thing I'll never do is fall down – or speak in tongues,' I would lovingly say that you probably will never experience this joy until you are *willing* for God to do what he pleases in you. As for tongues – possibly the greatest stigma of the Spirit to so many of us – we must not be afraid or defensive regarding this. I am not entirely sure why there is such a stigma (offence) attached to speaking in tongues. It may have something to do with people who are most associated with this phenomena (like Pentecostals), and we don't want to be seen around them or appear like them. Or it may have more to do with the embarrassment that comes with tongues. My very first reaction that followed my own speaking in tongues was, simply, feeling embarrassed despite the joy. At bottom, in my opinion, we delay what God would do in us because of sheer pride, or fear of what people might think. You may never speak in tongues or fall to the floor, but you must be willing to – if you want pure joy.

The embarrassment we want so much to avoid will be the very thing that we will feel most when exposed at the judgement seat of Christ. Here on earth we worry about a handful of people, often only one or two; at God's judgement we will have many watching – possibly everybody we ever knew! He or she that is faithful in that which is least (not worrying about a handful of observers) will be faithful in what is far greater (with many watching). And he or she who is unjust or unrighteous in that which is least will be the same in 'much' (Luke 16:10, AV). In other words, the pain of embarrassment will be multiplied when you face the Lord at his final judgement. What is more, there is the grief that will come because of our Lord's displeasure.

Pure joy is promised to all, but it is only received by those who want God and the offence of the cross more than anything in the world. God is a jealous God; he shares his joy with those who honour him and embrace the stigma.

Do you want pure joy? How much do you want it? This joy is nothing else than God himself. He wants to be real to you. Here is what I recommend to you if this joy is lacking: (1) be sure that you have totally forgiven anyone who has hurt you or been unjust to you in any way; (2) embrace any stigma that is associated with the Spirit so that you are utterly willing to look like a fool to those who know you; (3) dignify any and every trial God puts in your path; (4) seek the honour that comes from him rather than getting your ego massaged by the praise of people; and (5) seek his face by praying with all your heart – until this joy is yours.

Let us not become weary in doing good, for at the proper time we will reap a harvest if we do not give up. (Galatians 6:9)

So do not throw away your confidence; it will be richly rewarded. You need to persevere so that when you have done the will of God, you will receive what he has promised. For in just a very little while, 'He who is coming will come and will not delay'. (Heb. 10:35–7)

6

Flowing in the Spirit

Since we live by the Spirit, let us keep in step with the
Spirit. (Galatians 5:25)

I am sometimes asked if we can manifest the fruits of the
Spirit without having received the baptism of the Spirit.
Answer: yes. This is because we are all responsible for
showing the fruits of the Spirit in our lives. '. . . the fruit of
the Spirit is love, joy, peace, patience, kindness, goodness,
faithfulness, gentleness and self-control' (Gal. 5:22–3). We
all have the potential to manifest the fruits of the Spirit
because we have the Holy Spirit. Every Christian has the
Spirit of Christ. If one does not have the Spirit of Christ it
is because he or she does not belong to Christ (Rom. 8:9).
Therefore let no one say, 'I cannot demonstrate the fruits of
the Spirit because I have not received the baptism of the
Spirit.' All of us have not only the potential to show the

Spirit's fruits, but have a mandate from the Lord to do so.

I have been equally asked if we can witness for the Lord if we have not received the power promised in Acts 1:8, 'But you will receive power when the Holy Spirit comes on you; and you will be my witnesses . . .' Again the answer is: yes. We are responsible for sharing the gospel with others whether or not we have received the same kind of power given to the 120 in the upper room. The woman of Samaria was excited to tell the people in her area about Jesus. 'Come, see a man who told me everything I ever did. Could this be the Christ?' They came out of the town and made their way towards him. There is no indication that she had unusual power, only the joy of having met the Lord.

There is no doubt that the baptism of the Spirit helps in both of these areas. One of the fruits of the Spirit is joy and anyone who is baptised with the Spirit will know this joy. Power for witnessing is released by the baptism of the Spirit. This is, in fact, one of the purposes of the baptism or sealing of the Spirit. Not only is this the highest form of assurance; it enables one to witness with more effectiveness.

The strange irony is that someone can be baptised by the Spirit and later lose the joy, while someone who has not been baptised by the Spirit can experience this joy. The reason is this. Bitterness, or the absence of it, is very relevant to whether we flow in the Spirit. Not showing forgiveness to those who have hurt us is therefore very relevant to whether we flow in the Spirit. For the person who has totally forgiven his or her offenders will know pure joy. It is an inner release we feel once we have set totally free those people who have hurt us. And yet let no one say, 'I cannot totally forgive because I have not been baptised by the Spirit.' We are told to pray to be forgiven in proportion to our having forgiven others (Matt. 6:12). We are commanded to forgive our enemies and those who have hurt us, regardless of whether we have been baptised by the Spirit.

The issue therefore is developing sensitivity to the Spirit. This is done by *not grieving* him. The Holy Spirit is a person – a very sensitive person indeed. Paul said, '. . . do not grieve the Holy Spirit of God, with whom you were sealed for the day of redemption' (Eph. 4:30). The word translated 'grieve' comes from a word that means to get your feelings hurt. When a Christian hurts the Holy Spirit's feelings it does not mean we lose our salvation. For Paul even said that the Spirit seals us for the day of redemption! Nothing can be clearer than that. We are eternally secure by the Spirit's seal, and this sealing, though not necessarily consciously experienced at the moment of conversion, is none the less part of the package of being a Christian (1 Cor. 1:7). The conscious sealing of the Spirit is the result of the baptism of the Spirit, for the baptism of the Spirit gives us an infallible witness of what is true with regard to our security in Christ. Therefore when we grieve the Spirit, which all of us have done, it does not forfeit being saved. Praise God for that!

But something does happen when we grieve the Holy Spirit: not the loss of salvation, but presence of mind. I like to call it *presence of the mind of the Spirit*. The Holy Spirit is depicted in the New Testament as a dove (Matt. 3:16,

John 1:32). The dove is a very shy bird and extremely sensitive. I deal with this in some detail in *Sensitivity of the Spirit*. When the Spirit is grieved he backs away, as it were, like a dove that quietly and unobtrusively flies away. The result of this is that we are not able to flow in the Spirit as long as the Spirit is grieved and the Dove is not around.

The main way we grieve the Spirit is by bitterness and unforgiveness. We know this is true because the very next thing Paul says (after commanding us not to grieve the Spirit) is, 'Get rid of all bitterness, rage and anger, brawling and slander, along with every form of malice. Be kind and compassionate to one another, forgiving each other, just as in Christ God forgave you' (Eph. 4:31–2). Bitterness is not the only way we grieve the Spirit, and Paul continues to show what else grieves the Spirit: sexual immorality, greed, obscenity, foolish talk or coarse joking (Eph. 5:3–4). But bitterness is the chief way we grieve the Spirit, and that is why he puts it at the top of the list of things we can do to grieve the Spirit.

This means that all of us are accountable to God to forgive and to make sure the Holy Spirit is *ungrieved* in our hearts and lives. And when the Holy Spirit in us is ungrieved – like the dove coming down and remaining (see John 1:32–3) – we will (1) show the fruits of the Spirit (2) be able to witness for Jesus with power, and (3) flow in the Spirit.

What does flowing in the Spirit mean? It is moving along with him, keeping in step with him, and missing nothing he may be wanting to do through us. The joy of flowing in the Spirit is equal to anything God may ever do for us and in us.

There is such a thrill in flowing in the Spirit. You feel what you are doing is worthwhile; you feel authenticated, you feel loved; you know you are a part of something very important – the kingdom of God. It happens to me when I am preparing a sermon, witnessing to an unsaved person, helping my wife clean the house, doing the shopping, or anything else in life that is either necessary or a blessing to people. You feel this when visiting a sick person or resisting temptation; when you walk to work or do work in the office. It is a twenty-four hour a day possibility.

This is what Peter and John were doing when they were walking towards the temple one afternoon, but were unexpectedly stopped – only to see the healing of a forty-year-old man who had never walked (see Acts 3:1–10). There are two questions that emerge: (1) why were these disciples led at this particular time to administer healing to this man, and (2) how did they know this man would suddenly be healed? As to the first question, have you ever wondered why Jesus himself did not heal this man? After all, Jesus walked in and out of the temple – right past this beggar – countless times over the previous three years. Why didn't Jesus heal him? Could Jesus have healed him had he chosen to?

For all I know, Jesus wanted to heal the man long before the man received his healing at the hands of Peter and John. We don't know whether this is true, though; we only know that Jesus went past him without healing him. I have heard it said, 'If Jesus comes into your house he will bless you – fix anything that needs fixing, heal if that is what is needed.' Really? Jesus came right by this man, but did not heal him. Why not?

Believe it or not, Jesus was not his 'own man'. He said so. 'I tell you the truth, the Son can do nothing by himself; he can do only what he sees his Father doing, because whatever the Father does the Son also does' (John 5:19). Jesus took orders from the Father. Everything Jesus said or did was mirroring or repeating what the Father granted to be said or done. Jesus may well have wanted to heal the man at the Gate Beautiful. Or perhaps the Father said to him, 'I'm saving him for Peter and John'. What we do know is, the man was not healed until this point.

God is sovereign, and a missing note in teaching and preaching today is this very aspect about God. The sovereignty of God refers mainly to his will and power. God has a will of his own – independent of his creation – and that will needs to be affirmed and honoured for whatever he does or does not do. 'I will have mercy on whom I will have mercy, and I will have compassion on whom I will have compassion' (Exod. 33:19). In other words, God the Father was behind the decision not to heal this man during Jesus's days on earth, but equally behind the reason Peter and John were the chosen instruments to grant healing at this particular time.

And yet there is to be seen an equally important teaching regarding the Holy Spirit: he too only does what the Father tells him to do. Jesus and the Holy Spirit in this sense are identical because both the Son and the Spirit carry out the Father's wishes – and nothing more. All that Jesus ever did, and all that the Holy Spirit ever does, is sovereignly orches- trated by the Father in heaven. John 5:19, quoted above, anticipates the exact same truth about the Holy Spirit. Jesus said that the Holy Spirit 'will not speak on his own; he will speak only what he hears' (John 16:13). This goes to show that the Holy Spirit, like Jesus, does nothing by himself, but only what he hears from the Father. Therefore the Holy Spirit was sovereignly at work, carrying out the Father's will, when Peter and John came upon this man at the temple gate. That is the only explanation for the healing right then, and not before.

But now to the second question: how did Peter and John *know* that this man's time had come and that the Spirit was willing to perform this wonderful miracle? Answer: they had the joy of flowing in the Spirit. Peter and John stopping to address the lame man was not their idea; it was the Spirit's idea. The time of this man's healing had come. Peter and John were privileged to be a part of the Father's plan at such a time as this.

But the question still remains: how did they know that God was going to do this and work through them at that particular moment? It was because they were walking in the *ungrieved* Spirit; the heavenly Dove was remaining on them. I reckon that if they had left home with an unresolved argument with their wives, the Dove would have flown away and they would not have experienced the sovereign impulse of the Spirit. Had they been in a heated argument with each other as they approached the temple, they would not have felt the Spirit's impulse. What if John had interrupted Peter as he was addressing the handicapped man, 'Why is it always you who speaks first – why can't I speak first once in a while?', the Dove would have surely disappeared. The easiest thing in the world to do is to grieve the Spirit, and the extent of his sensitivity cannot be exaggerated. But Peter and John were enjoying sweet fellowship with the Spirit and with each other. They were keeping in step with the Spirit and so they did not miss out on what God was prepared to do. It gave them great joy to be involved in this miracle.

If the question is asked, 'If the time of the man's miracle had come and it was what God willed to do, how could Peter and John miss out on this by causing the Dove to fly away?' All I know for sure is, Peter and John were ready. They had been trained by Jesus and had learned much about the ways of the Spirit. They didn't miss out. Luke does not record what goes on behind the scenes when it comes to the ways of the Spirit and the sovereignty of God. Nothing takes God by surprise. I only know that the Holy Spirit can be quenched (1 Thess. 5:19), which means that he may withdraw from working – at least for the moment. God's purpose will not ultimately be overturned. He may, however, choose a *different* instrument should those of us who are smug and insensitive to the Spirit become unteachable. Jesus warned the church at Ephesus that if they did not return to their first love, he would remove their candlestick from its place (Rev. 2:5). This is why for centuries God has been in the habit of raising up movements outside the establishment that would be obedient when traditional Christians would not.

Hundreds of years before Pentecost there had been servants of God who flowed in the Spirit. I am sure this was what Jonathan and his armour-bearer experienced when they were instruments of God in a great feat. Jonathan said to his armour-bearer, 'Come, let's go over to the outpost of those uncircumcised fellows. Perhaps the LORD will act on our behalf. Nothing can hinder the LORD from saving, whether by many or by few' (1 Sam. 14:6). His armour-bearer replied, 'Do all that you have in mind . . . I am with you heart and soul' (v. 7). This is called the unity of the Spirit (Eph. 4:3; Phil. 2:1). It is when the ungrieved Spirit in me and the ungrieved Spirit in you enable the Spirit – and us – to work in harmony together. How can two walk together in this fashion unless they are in agreement?

Flowing in the Spirit means to honour God's 'no' as well as his 'yes', the red light as well as the green light. Paul and his companions were 'kept by the Holy Spirit' ('forbidden', AV) from preaching the word in the province of Asia (Acts 16:6). Really? Are we to believe that the *Holy Spirit* – not the devil – would actually stop people from preaching the gospel? It seems to me that this would take both supernatural discernment and considerable courage to act on a word from the Spirit like that. This seems to fly in the face of our mandate to preach the gospel to every person (Mark 16:15). But that is what was happening. Did not these people need the gospel? Yes. Then why were they forbidden by the Spirit from preaching in Asia at this time? You tell me. I only know they listened to the Spirit and obeyed. It must have taken as much courage to obey not to preach as it did to preach it. How did they know? I only know that they knew. To flow in the Spirit is to have intimacy with him and to feel what he wants.

Not only that; when they came to the border of Mysia

and tried to enter Bithynia, 'the Spirit of Jesus would not allow them to' (Acts 16:7). Had this been a providential hindrance – or opposition – Luke would have said so. Paul wanted to come to Rome, but said he was prevented many times (Rom. 1:13) and claimed to be stopped by Satan from coming to Thessalonica (1 Thess. 2:18). But both incidents in the book of Acts attribute their course of direction to the Holy Spirit. Paul and his companions walked in the Spirit because they knew his *ways*.

God lamented of ancient Israel, '. . . they have not known my ways' (Heb. 3:10). To flow in the Spirit is to learn God's ways, his style, his manner of doing things, his way with people, his gentleness, his indignation, his impulses. In a word: what pleases the Spirit and what he prompts you to do. God wants us to know his ways; it is as though God admits to having a certain kind of personality. He wants us to adjust to his ways. You get to know a person's ways by spending time with them. My wife Louise and I have been married for forty-five years. I know her ways, she knows mine. When we are asked a question or receive an invitation, we almost always know what the other will say. God wants us to know him like that. But Israel didn't know him like that and it made God unhappy. He swore an oath that they would never enter into his rest (Heb. 4:3). God wants intimacy with us and there is no greater joy than to keep in step with the Spirit.

I have referred to Louise's big change as a result of the ministry of Rodney Howard-Browne. It used to irk her a bit when she heard me call for all members of Westminster Chapel to spend at least thirty minutes a day in prayer alone.

She felt this was unfair to them. 'How can you ask people to spend that much time alone in prayer? Most people run out of things to pray for after a few minutes.' But after she was touched by the Holy Spirit she wanted to spend more and more time talking with him – in solitude. She now feels cheated if she doesn't get at least a whole hour with him alone every single day, and regards two hours as far better. Believe me, I am not exaggerating. Once she tasted the deep communion with the Spirit and intimacy with him – and experiencing him talking to her – she was absolutely spoiled.

Jesus referred to his 'joy' (John 15:11, 17:13). The source of that joy was partly knowing that he pleased the Father and had his Father's approval (see Matt. 3:17, 17:5, John 8:29), and Jesus's prayer life cannot be separated from this. Jesus was a man of prayer. When did he pray? All the time. But he needed to be alone as well. According to Mark, Jesus preferred mornings (Mark 1:35). According to Matthew, Jesus prayed in the evening – by himself (Matt. 14:23). According to Luke, he prayed all night (Luke 6:13)! One must never doubt the joy he received from the time he had alone with the Father.

How much do you pray? There will be no praying in heaven. We may regret many things at the judgement seat of Christ – how we used our time, how we spent our money, the friends we chose, the decisions we made; but I can safely promise you one thing you will not regret: the time you spent alone with the Lord. The joy of flowing in the Spirit twenty-four hours a day is traceable or connected in some way to the time spent alone with the Lord. If Jesus, who was the Son of God and was filled with the Spirit without limit

(John 3:34), felt the need to do this, how much more do you and I need it?

What one wants to do when praying alone is to *pray in the Spirit*. Paul uses this expression in the context of spiritual warfare. Towards the end of Ephesians 6 is that classic passage that tells us we wrestle not against flesh and blood, but against Satan – the power of this dark world and spiritual forces of evil in the heavenly realms (Eph. 6:12). We are told what to do:

> Therefore put on the full armour of God, so that when the day of evil comes, you may be able to stand your ground, and after you have done everything, to stand. Stand firm then, with the belt of truth buckled round your waist, with the breastplate of righteousness in place, and with your feet fitted with the readiness that comes from the gospel of peace. In addition to all this, take up the shield of faith, with which you can extinguish all the flaming arrows of the evil one. Take the helmet of salvation and the sword of the Spirit, which is the word of God. (vv. 13–17)

But then comes this phrase to *pray in the Spirit*. It is tucked away towards the end of this section, and because Paul does not use metaphors, it is easy to think he has changed the subject somewhat. No. Praying in the Spirit is a vital part of spiritual warfare. Jude uses the same expression in his little epistle: '. . . build yourselves up in your most holy faith and pray in the Holy Spirit' (Jude 20). This seems to be what Paul means in Romans 8:26: '. . . the Spirit helps us in our weakness. We do not know what we ought to pray for, but the Spirit himself intercedes for us with groans that words cannot express.'

Flowing in the Spirit is praying in the Spirit. Praying in the Spirit is praying in the will of God. It is the only kind of praying that matters because it is only when we ask in God's will that we are heard. We are fools if we think we can upstage God's will, as if our idea would be better than his. Here is a principle you can count on for the rest of your life: God always gives his best to those who leave the choice with him. The reason is this. He already has a plan for you. It has been carefully thought out. The same wisdom that entered into God's plan for creation and redemption is the brilliance and care that lay behind his thoughts towards you. He has lavished the riches of his grace with wisdom and understanding (Eph. 1:7–8). As David put it: '*How precious to me are your thoughts, O God! How vast is the sum of them! Were I to count them, they would outnumber the grains of sand*' (Ps. 139:17–18).

God's plan for us was designed before we were born, while still in our mother's womb (Ps. 139:13); indeed, from the foundation of the world (Eph. 1:4,11). This is why only a fool would try to come up with a better idea than the one already conceived in God's heart and mind. Therefore to pray in the will of God is the best thing we can do when it comes to prayer. To flow in the Spirit is to flow in God's will and to pray in God's will.

However, praying in the Spirit, or praying in God's will, is carried out at one of two levels (or perhaps both): (1) when you know what God's will is and pray accordingly; or

(2) when you don't know what God's will is but pray with groans that words cannot express – that is, words you don't understand. The first level is, in my opinion, quite rare. It does not happen to me every day. It has happened, but not often. It is when I *know* somehow that when I pray for something I also know God heard me and that it will be answered because I was given to know that I just prayed in the will of God. It is a joyous feeling. Jesus referred to this when he said, '. . . whatever you ask for in prayer, believe that you have received it, and it will be yours' (Mark 11:24). I wish I could say that I engage in this kind of praying all the time. I do not know why God will not let me pray in the Spirit like this more often. I do know, though, that Jesus added a word here that could easily be forgotten: 'And when you stand praying, if you hold anything against anyone, forgive him, so that your Father in heaven may forgive you your sins' (Mark 11:25).

It may be that more of us would pray consciously in the will of God more often than we do if there was truly total forgiveness towards all people as we pray. But even so, when I really do believe I have totally forgiven others, I cannot say I pray in God's will – at least in English – very often. I am *willing* to do so, but I usually do not know for sure that what I am asking is in God's will. Zechariah and Elizabeth prayed for a son. They did not know that they put this request in God's will and that it was *heard* (that means received in heaven as a request that will be granted). But it was – except that they were not notified for a long time. One day, unexpectedly, the angel Gabriel appeared to Zechariah and said, '. . . your prayer has been heard. Your wife Elizabeth will bear you a son, and you are to give him the name John' (Luke 1:13). Zechariah wanted to argue with Gabriel (a rather stupid thing to do!) as if to say, 'You've made a mistake. My wife is too old for this now' (Luke 1:18). In any case, the prayer was answered!

The point is this. Zechariah had prayed years before in the will of God but was not given the grace of the Spirit to *know at the time* he was praying in God's will. Knowing at the time is therefore, in my view, rare. However, John admits to the possibility when he says, 'And *if we know that he hears us* [a big 'if', and my italics] – whatever we ask – we know that we have what we asked of him' (1 John 5:15). This level of praying in the Spirit is when you think and pray in your mother tongue.

This brings us to the second level of praying in the Spirit. It is when you *do* pray in the will of God, but you do not know what you are praying for. How can this be? It is almost certainly praying in tongues. Romans 8:26, quoted above, coheres with 1 Corinthians 14:2: 'For anyone who speaks in a tongue does not speak to men but to God. Indeed, no-one understands him; he utters mysteries with his spirit.' When you are praying in this manner you are praying in the will of God. This is why I said above that you could pray consciously in the will of God at both levels. This is because when I pray in tongues I abandon my wishes to the Spirit. I do not know what God's will is, true, but I know none the less that I am praying in God's will because I am praying in tongues. I am praying in the Spirit, flowing in the Spirit.

I had an unforgettable experience in Kenya when Michael Eaton and I were being entertained by His Excellency

Daniel arap Moi, then the President of Kenya. Michael was not aware of it, although I told him later. I found myself struggling to pray particular things, and wanted to make sure I got certain things said to God (in case he would forget!), when I felt a loving rebuke by the Holy Spirit: 'Don't you realise that when you pray in tongues you will have all you need, for God will cause you to pray for the need, if it is a need.' It slightly embarrassed me, but it gave me no small comfort. I have learned from that experience and have sought to pray in tongues more and more often because that way I know I am praying in the Spirit and thus in God's will. I leave things to him this way. However, it would be a mistake to pray only in tongues. Paul went on to say in 1 Corinthians that he prayed in the Spirit, but also with his *mind* (1 Cor. 14:15). I pray more with my mind (thinking and speaking in English) than I do in tongues, but I know that when I pray in tongues I am praying in God's will, for the Holy Spirit does the effectual interceding in God's will (Rom. 8:27).

Praying in tongues is not always pure joy. The joy is knowing you are getting it right because the Holy Spirit becomes the effective intercessor. One may even have a spirit of heaviness as one prays in tongues. Some who do not pray in tongues suppose that it is a rapturous experience to pray in tongues, and it certainly can be. Sometimes there is a spontaneous flow of unintelligible syllables and sounds that you would hope nobody will hear! It is praise in the Spirit and can be wonderful. But when you are carrying a burden and pray in tongues, it does not mean that the burden goes away.

Very recently when I arrived at Miami airport and phoned Louise to say that I was starting to drive home, she shared an urgent need and wondered if I would pray hard on my way home to Key Largo (a little over an hour's drive). I did. I decided to pray in tongues all the way home. I felt nothing except heaviness, but knew in my heart it was not for nothing. A few minutes before arriving home I felt a lifting of my spirit and concluded I could, and should, stop praying, so I did. I then left the matter to God. I can tell you, within twenty-four hours the situation completely changed regarding the person I prayed for. I was not surprised. God answers prayer, and when we pray in the Spirit we are not only flowing in the Spirit but praying in God's will.

Flowing in the Spirit is the best way to live. This is not to say that one is conscious all the time that he or she is flowing in the Spirit. But one can be fairly certain whether the Holy Spirit resides in a person *ungrieved*, and when we know this is the case, there is great peace and an absence of tension and anxiety.

There are, however, unusual times of flowing in the Spirit. That is when God is up to something that is not your usual everyday happening. Most of life is what Richard Bewes calls 'between the times' – the relatively unexciting period between the mountain-top experiences. Most of life is lived not on the mountain-top, but in the valley. When Jesus was transfigured before his closest disciples high on a mountain, Peter said, 'Lord, it is good for us to be here' and began to make suggestions on how to stay there! But shortly after-wards they came down the mountain where life is to be lived (Matt. 17:1–9). And yet we must learn to flow in the

Spirit in the valley as well as during those times when God does the unusual.

At Westminster Chapel we made some important decisions and some of them had to do with inviting guest speakers like Arthur Blessitt, Billy Graham, Paul Cain, John Arnott and Rodney Howard-Browne. Often I would preach a special sermon – breaking into the series I happened to be in – to prepare our people for the unusual. (This in itself would make for an interesting book!) In those days I experienced flowing in the Spirit at what I would call a high level. When I was set to invite Arthur Blessitt I felt an intense excitement and leading to have him, unlike anything I had ever known. When I made the decision to begin Pilot Lights (witnessing on the streets) I felt fire in my bones. The same sort of thing occurred at critical times in our twenty-five years at Westminster Chapel, as when the Toronto Blessing came to the Chapel and how I prepared our people. In those days I knew I was flowing in the Spirit. I can tell you that I have not regretted a single decision ever made in those twenty-five years when I felt I was flowing in the Spirit. Moreover, the same thing occurred when I felt led to announce our retirement and when I recommended Greg Haslam to follow me. God has never – ever – let me down or left me with the feeling I had been deceived when I experienced flowing in the Spirit. It was pure joy, although sometimes it can be costly. You may lose some friends because you are misunderstood. But God never deserts us.

A marvellous example of flowing in the Spirit was the way Paul reacted to a demon-possessed girl who kept pursuing him. The young lady had a gift of predicting the future and was into fortune telling. Mocking Paul and his companions, she kept shouting, 'These men are servants of the Most High God, who are telling you the way to be saved.' The funny thing was, she was telling the truth. The Puritan William Perkins would say, 'Don't believe the devil even when he tells the truth.' What strikes me was Paul's patience with the girl. Many of us today might jump in at once and confront this girl, who was obviously a disturbance to their ministry. She kept up the shouting for many days. Finally, Paul became so troubled that he turned around and said to the malicious spirit, 'In the name of Jesus Christ I command you to come out of her!' At that moment the spirit left her (Acts 16:16–18). When we flow in the Spirit we reflect God's timing: never too late, never too early, but always just on time.

The incident of the exorcism of the girl resulted in Paul and Silas being put in prison, and there too they flowed in the Spirit as they sang praises to God. When the authorities realised that Paul was a Roman citizen and had been imprisoned without a trial, they were alarmed and keen to set them free and send them on their way. 'No,' said Paul in so many words. 'You will treat us with dignity and respect and escort us out of town' (Acts 16: 25–40). Paul was still flowing in the Spirit when he stood by a just principle.

When Paul was in Athens his 'spirit was stirred' (Acts 17:16, AV) when he noted the idolatry around the city. He was supposedly 'between the times' because he was only there to wait for Timothy. But he went to the market place and began to witness to 'those who happened to be there' (Acts 17:17), a verse that always encouraged me when we took to the streets in London every Saturday. The decision to go to the market place and witness for the Lord led to a prestigious invitation for Paul – to address the learned philosophers of Athens. There he addressed them and Luke records a summary of his sermon and the results (Acts 17:24–34). This would not have occurred had Paul not kept in step with the Spirit by using the time to witness. Sometimes what we think may be 'between the times' can turn out to be epochal. Speaking personally, what we did at Westminster Chapel in the spring of 1982 – when I invited Arthur Blessitt and began our Pilot Light ministry – turned out to be the most important decision I made in my twenty-five years there. I could not have known it would close doors, but also open others which, as it happened, gave me a wider ministry than I had ever had before.

In June 2002 a man I hardly knew said that my forth-coming trip to Israel would result in my making an impact over there that was not connected to the tour I was planning to help lead. Although Paul told us not to treat prophecies with contempt (1 Thess. 5:20), I fear I came close to doing just that as I hardly took the man seriously, although he spoke with what I would call an almost extreme earnestness and conviction. Two weeks later I flew into Tel Aviv and was picked up by an Arab driver who took me to a hotel in Jerusalem. As a result of a conversation with him, I was phoned several days later – the day after the tour was over – by Andrew White, canon of Coventry Cathedral and the Archbishop of Canterbury's envoy to the Middle East. I casually told the Arab driver that I had begun praying for Yasser Arafat every day in 1982 because of things Arthur

Blessitt had told me about his own meeting with Arafat. While this Palestinian driver – whose name is Osama – began making phone calls to see if he could get me a meeting with Yasser Arafat, I related this conversation to Julia Fisher of Premier Radio, who organised the tour, and she then told Andrew White, who happened to fly into Israel the day after the tour ended. Andrew White told me he had just read my book *Total Forgiveness* and that his parents attended our School of Theology on Friday nights at Westminster Chapel. Osama was not able to work things out with the Israeli government for me to meet Arafat, but Andrew White, probably the only man in the world who has the trust of Yasser Arafat and the Israeli government, said he would phone back.

'Yasser Arafat will see you at 6 o'clock tomorrow evening,' said Andrew White. We met at our hotel at 5 p.m. the next day to be briefed. I would have left Israel when the rest of the people in our tour party flew back had not my friends Lyndon Bowring and Alan Bell come to see me there – on the very day the others all left – to have a few days of relaxation. Andrew got permission for both Alan and Lyndon to join me in Arafat's compound in Ramallah.

I never dreamed of meeting Yasser Arafat. 'God moves in a mysterious way his wonders to perform,' wrote William Cowper. But with precious little time to prepare or think about it, there we were sitting with Yasser Arafat and three of his cabinet ministers. Lyndon and Alan chose not to speak, but promised to pray constantly the whole time – quietly in tongues – as I spoke to the Chairman of the Palestinian Liberation Organisation. Andrew said that most visits with Arafat last about twenty minutes, but for some reason we found ourselves in the compound for nearly two hours. We had one hour and forty-five minutes with Arafat himself . . . talking almost the entire time about Jesus. Nothing else. 'I come not as a politician, but as a follower of Jesus Christ,' I said to Arafat after he kissed me on both cheeks. We connected, and I will tell you the reason: Lyndon and Alan gave me a particular bit of advice and, as I said, prayed for me the whole time. I can tell you that I had as much – if not more – anointing to speak to Yasser Arafat as I have had in any sermon I ever preached at Westminster Chapel. How much good we did I would not want to say, but I know one thing: it was a case of flowing in the Spirit in Arafat's compound in Ramallah. If I had the whole time to do it all over again, I would not change a word I said. What Arafat felt I cannot be sure, but he heard the gospel. I emphasised no fewer than six times that Jesus *died* on the cross, and was not taken straight to heaven as Arafat wanted to say. Two of the cabinet ministers profusely thanked us for coming. 'You cheered him up,' they said, but I had hoped to see him converted. Whatever, it was a contrast to the eerie sound of the Muslim call to prayer that fell on Ramallah as we waited for clearance to leave. When we walk in the Spirit, all we can do is leave the rest to God.

Flowing in the Spirit is the best way to live. It is the way that God wants all his people to live. We never know when our time will come. You may think you are merely 'between the times', but God can turn the day of seemingly small things into an event that changes everything around you.

'It's not over till it's over,' as Yogi Berra used to say. What God does for us, in us and through us, when we flow in the Spirit is not always for us to know. What happens is what comes out when we stand before the Lord on that Day of days.

7

The Judgement Seat
of Christ

> For we must all appear before the judgement seat of Christ, that each one may receive what is due to him for the things done while in the body, whether good or bad. (2 Corinthians 5:10)

I was brought up in the hills of Kentucky. In our church in Ashland, Kentucky, we often had visiting preachers and evangelists, with varying degrees of erudition, ignorance and education. But nearly all of them had in common a belief that there is a heaven and a hell. Some would preach heaven with such eloquence that you could hardly wait to get there, and some would preach on hell to the point where you could almost smell the brimstone.

We were in what I would call the 'tail end' of the spiritual momentum begun by the Cane Ridge revival in Bourbon County, Kentucky, over 100 miles away, back in 1802. If America's first Great Awakening is symbolised by Jonathan Edwards's immortal sermon 'Sinners in the Hands of an Angry God' in 1741, the Cane Ridge revival – called the 'Second Great Awakening' by historians – was sparked off by somewhat similar preaching. This explains why I heard the kind of preaching I did as a child and why I have continued to be influenced by it. I have not accepted my theological heritage uncritically, however. The proof of this was my moving away from the theology of my old denomination when it came to doctrines of salvation and grace. But for some reason I have not been able to shake off the teaching and preaching of eternal punishment. I still find it interesting that both of these movements of the Spirit, one that began in New England and the other that started the tradition of 'camp meetings', were characterised by the preaching of the justice and mercy of God.

Here is what happened at Cane Ridge. A Methodist lay preacher who said that he had no invitation to preach decided to preach anyway. He found a fallen tree and stood on it. He wrote:

I commenced reading a hymn with an audible voice, and by the time we concluded singing and praying we had around us, standing on their feet, by fair calculation 10,000 people. I gave out my text . . . 'For we must all stand before the Judgement Seat of Christ' and before I concluded my voice was not to be heard for the groans of the distressed and the shouts of triumph. Hundreds fell prostrate to the ground, and the work of conversion continued on that spot until Wednesday afternoon. It was estimated by some that not less than 500 were at one time lying on the ground with deepest agonies of distress, and every few minutes rising in shouts of triumph.

At the end of the day the teaching that will be found to have motivated me the most – my life and doctrine – is 2 Corinthians 5:10: 'For we must all appear before the judgement seat of Christ, that each one may receive what is due to him for the things done while in the body, whether good or bad.' I am incapable of describing adequately how deep this verse runs inside me and how vividly it flows through my spiritual and theological veins. It is the scariest and most thrilling verse I know of next to the gospel itself. It tells me that, even though I am eternally and unchangeably saved, I must none the less give an account of my whole life – before the Lord, the angels and, almost certainly, all who ever knew me.

There are certain theological premises and principles that need to be outlined early in this chapter so that the reader can understand what we are talking about. I will state the teaching and elaborate more fully later in the chapter.

1   *Judgement follows the second coming of Jesus.* 'Just as man is destined to die once, and after that to face judgement, so Christ was sacrificed once to take away the sins of many people; and he will appear a second time, not to

bear sin, but to bring salvation to those who are waiting for him' (Heb. 9:27–8).

I will not enter into the issue of all that happens just before or just after the second coming. The issue of the millennium is controversial and there is no point in trying to resolve it in this book. The point is, some time after Jesus returns he will be seated on a 'great white throne' (Rev. 20:11). He himself said he would one day be judge, because in the Sermon on the Mount he claimed that 'Many will say to *me* [my italics] on that day, "Lord, Lord, did we not prophesy in your name, and in your name drive out demons and perform many miracles?" Then I will tell them plainly, "I never knew you. Away from me, you evildoers"' (Matt. 7:22–3). At Athens Paul preached that God would judge the world by 'the man he has appointed' – Jesus (Acts 17:31). Indeed, Christ 'will judge the living and the dead' after his return (2 Tim. 4:1).

2   *The final judgement will deal with who is saved and who is lost.* 'The angels will come and separate the wicked from the righteous and throw them into the fiery furnace, where there will be weeping and gnashing of teeth' (Matt. 13:49–50). The lost will 'go away to eternal punishment, but the righteous to eternal life' (Matt. 25:46). It would seem that prior to this the devil will have been sent to hell (Rev. 20:10) and will then be joined by the lost.

The basis of this phase of the judgement will be who has trusted the Lord Jesus Christ for the forgiveness of sins and who has not. Those who have relied on Jesus and his death will be eternally saved, all others will perish. I cannot go into the details of what happens to those who have never heard the gospel, only that I concur with Billy Graham: they will be judged by a different standard. Peter commented that judgement begins with the family of God. Whether he was in any sense referring to the order at the final judgement, I do not know. If he was, then it may turn out that the saved are judged first. In any case, Peter said, '. . . if it begins with us, what will the outcome be for those who do not obey the gospel of God?' (1 Pet. 4:17).

3   *Those who are saved will also be judged.* This aspect of the final judgement is what Paul is referring to when he says in 2 Corinthians 5:10 that 'we' shall all stand before the judgement seat of Christ. I take the 'we' to refer to the saved. If he means all people, this too fits the verse. But it really refers to the redeemed of the Lord, who will give an account of their lives. Paul immediately stated that the thought of the judgement seat of Christ impacted him in his own life and motivated him to reach the lost. 'Knowing therefore the terror of the Lord, we persuade men' (2 Cor. 5:11, AV). This shows that one of the purposes of the teaching of the judgement seat of Christ is to affect our lives now so that we will be prepared for that awesome event.

The word translated 'judgement' in this verse comes from the Greek word *bema*. The Bema Seat in the ancient Hellenistic world was the place – always in public view and out in the open – where rewards and punishments were meted out. Winners in the Olympics appeared before the Bema Seat to receive their garland or crown. Likewise, punishments for wrong-doings were given here. We can go to Corinth today and see how archaeologists have uncovered the ancient Bema Seat there, and re-built it so that we can have some idea of what it was like. Paul chose this word when he wanted to refer to the final judgement – the *bema*. This judgement will not deal with whether you are saved or lost. This is the final judgement for the saved.

4   *It will be revealed at the judgement seat of Christ whether one receives a reward or is rejected for such a reward.* All whose sins are forgiven by faith in the blood of Christ will be saved and go to heaven, but not all who are saved and go to heaven will receive a reward at the judgement seat of Christ. Heaven and the receiving of a reward are not the same thing. All who are saved will have a home in heaven, but the reward is separate – *in addition* to the promise of heaven.

The reward – sometimes called 'prize', 'crown' or 'inheritance' – is promised to every believer, but the promise is conditional. This is why not all who are saved automatically receive a reward. Paul posed the sad possibility of a person truly saved, but who would 'suffer loss' – namely, the loss of reward that he or she might have received (1 Cor. 3:15). The apostle Paul was very concerned that he himself might not receive this reward, for God is impartial and no respecter of persons. 'No, I beat my body and make it my slave so that after I have preached to others, I myself will not be disqualified for the prize' (1 Cor. 9:27).

5   *The basis of the reward will be the quality of the superstructure that is over the foundation.* With any building there is first the foundation, and then comes what is erected on top of the foundation. Paul uses this analogy to depict salvation (the foundation) and rewards (what the super-structure is made of).

The foundation is Jesus Christ. '. . . no-one can lay any foundation other than the one already laid, which is Jesus Christ' (1 Cor. 3:11). If a person is resting on that foundation, he or she is saved. This is why Paul said that 'each one should be careful how he builds' (1 Cor. 3:10). Paul uses metaphors to show the materials that could make up the superstructure – gold, silver, costly stones, wood, hay or straw (1 Cor. 3:12). The superstructure therefore might be made of materials that are imperishable – like gold or precious stones; or what could be burned up – like wood or straw.

Obedience to the Lord Jesus, walking in the light, flowing in the Spirit and being unashamed of the stigma will mean building on the foundation with gold, silver and precious stones. These cannot be destroyed by fire. Indeed, they survive fire. But disobedience, being ashamed of the stigma, refusing to forgive or to dignify the trial God presents to us, will mean erecting a superstructure of wood, hay, straw. These will be burned up and will not survive fire.

6   *Fire will reveal the quality of the superstructure.* On this Day of days, to which all history is moving, each person's 'work will be shown for what it is, because the Day will bring it to light. It will be revealed with fire, and the fire

will test the quality of everyone's work' (1 Cor. 3:13). I do not know what kind of fire Paul is talking about, whether it is literal, supernatural or metaphorical fire. It may be fire referred to in 2 Thessalonians 1:7 – when Jesus is 'revealed from heaven in blazing fire'. What we do know is that the purpose of the fire is to burn up what can be burned, namely, wood, hay or straw. The fire that will be used at the judgement seat of Christ will 'test the quality' of every Christian's work – to see what survives.

We are not saved by works (Eph. 2:8–9), but the *reward* – or loss of reward – will be based on works. Dignifying the trial is a good work, but that is not how we are saved. Totally forgiving our enemies, or anyone who hurts us, is a beautiful work, but that is not how we are saved. We are saved by the sheer grace of God, but the reward is based upon a superstructure that will not perish when fire is put to it. When we endured suffering without grumbling, when we totally forgave those who were unkind or unjust, we may have thought that it went unnoticed. Wrong. The Day will bring it to light! Bearing the stigma and walking in the light, though it is costly, is building a superstructure of gold! Imagine gold, silver, precious stones, wood, hay and straw thrown in together on a solid foundation; then pour petrol on all of it and strike a match. What is left after the fire? Gold, silver, precious stones. The frail superstructure made of perishable materials will be utterly gone and out of the picture.

7   *If our superstructure survives the fire at the judgement seat of*

Christ, we will receive a reward. Paul says so: 'If what he has built survives, he will receive his reward' (1 Cor. 3:14). Every day you and I are erecting a superstructure. When we hold a grudge, we build a superstructure of wood, hay or straw. When we complain during a trial, it means a superstructure of what will perish in the heat of God's fiery judgement. When we are ashamed of the stigma we bear when we follow Christ or embrace the things of the Spirit that embarrass us, we build a perishable superstructure. Only the superstructure of gold or precious stones will survive the test that will be put to us at the Bema Seat of Christ.

This is another big 'if' – *if* what we have erected in our lives as Christians survives, we will receive that reward. The reward therefore is conditional, not automatic. All saved people will unconditionally go to heaven, but not all saved people will receive a reward. This is conditional, based on our walk with the Lord, our sensitivity and obedience to the Spirit, and our willingness to have moved outside our comfort zones when we wanted to be comfortable. When that Day comes, we will be so glad then that we endured the pain and accepted the cost of discipleship.

8   *Some Christians will lose the reward that could have been theirs because their superstructure will burn up at the judgement seat of Christ.* 'If it is burned up, he will suffer loss' (1 Cor. 3:15). The loss is not salvation or a home in heaven – thank God – but loss of reward. It was what Paul feared could happen to him, to be rejected for the 'prize' (1 Cor. 9:27). He admits to the possibility that

even an apostle could lose his reward in heaven. Amazing! What an embarrassment that would be. This is the very reason I have written – and preached for years – that I will not be surprised to observe weeping and gnashing of teeth among the saved at the judgement seat of Christ. They will see their folly, what they missed and could have been theirs – as well as observing what faithful Christians enjoy – right before their eyes.

Picture this. High-profile Christians – well-known personalities, perhaps ministers, vicars, bishops, arch-bishops, and who knows who or what else – having to suffer loss in front of all those who knew them here on earth. Paul was sure that it could happen to him. I can tell you candidly, I fear it could happen to me. Having a high profile here below is hardly a guarantee of a reward in heaven. If anything, it militates against it. The reason is this: we will be judged by a higher standard. Like it or not, that is the way it is. 'Not many of you should presume to be teachers, my brothers, because you know that we who teach will be judged more strictly' (Jas. 3:1). Jesus said, 'From everyone who has been given much, much will be demanded; and from the one who has been entrusted with much, much more will be asked' (Luke 12:48). I myself would be utterly with-out excuse. God has given me a head start – Christian parents, good upbringing, the best possible mentors, and being spared so much judgement from God that I have deserved. I sometimes fear the worst when I examine the kind of person I really ought to be. It is very scary indeed.

9   *The person who loses his or her reward will still be saved and go to heaven.* '. . . he himself will be saved, but only as one escaping through the flames' (1 Cor. 3:15). This verse further validates the teaching of once saved, always saved. There are good and sincere Christians who honestly believe – and fear – that if they are not fully obedient, or lapse in any way, they will forfeit the grace of God in salvation and will be lost if they do not repent before they die. I myself was brought up on this teaching. It is an awful way to have to live, to think that one could still go to hell at the end of the day if he or she does not come up to a high standard and maintain it.

It is my view that people who do not maintain such a standard will suffer loss, yes – loss of their reward at the judgement seat of Christ. But they will still be saved. Why? Because they remain on the foundation – Jesus Christ. The Authorised Version uses the expression 'saved by fire'. The reason is that the fire, although it burns up the superstructure, reveals that there was a foundation all along. The apostle Paul was not the slightest bit worried about losing his salvation, but he was unsure – at least at the time he wrote 1 Corinthians – of receiving a reward. But when he wrote 2 Timothy, almost certainly his final epistle just before he was beheaded in Rome, it was a rather different story:

I have fought the good fight, I have finished the race, I have kept the faith. Now there is in store for me the crown of righteousness, which the Lord, the right-eous Judge, will award to me on that day – and not only to me, but also to all who have longed for his appearing. (2 Timothy 4:7–8)

10 *Our permanent home in heaven is presented after the final judgement.* The judgement follows the second coming, but precedes our entrance into heaven. How much time elapses between the two events, I do not know. I base this teaching largely on the way heaven is presented in the book of Revelation. After John describes the great white throne and the consequence of not having your name written in the book of life (Rev. 20:11–15), he tells us what he then saw: 'a new heaven and a new earth' (Rev. 21:1). I would therefore put the scenario I have dealt with in the present chapter in this chronological order: (1) the second coming; (2) the judgement seat of Christ; and (3) our welcome into heaven.

This is important for us because many ask the question, 'How can a person be happy in heaven if he or she does not receive a reward at the judgement seat of Christ?' I answer: God will wipe away their tears. There will be no unhappiness in heaven – you can count on that. The dread and regret and the tears will be very real at the judgement seat of Christ – you can count on that as well – but after the rewards are bestowed and the divine gavel signals that the court's business is finished, God will graciously wipe away the tears. Indeed, 'He will wipe every tear from their eyes. There will be no more death or mourning or crying or pain, for the old order of things has passed away' (Rev. 21:4). There will be no unhappiness in heaven, only bliss. For ever.

Pure joy will be the experience of those who walk into heaven. It will be the sight of looking at Jesus who died on the cross for our sins. Jesus will be the only person in heaven with any kind of scar on his body. We know this because this is the way he was after being resurrected from the dead. Whereas you and I will be *changed* after death – transformed into glorified bodies (1 Cor. 15:52) – Jesus, though given a glorified body, still had the scars on his body. He said to Thomas, who protested that he would not believe that Jesus was truly risen unless he saw the very scars on his body, 'Put your finger here; see my hands. Reach out your hand and put it into my side' (John 20:27). Throughout eternity Jesus will for ever and ever keep those scars as a permanent reminder of how it was we all got there – by the shedding of his precious blood.

Pure joy will be what every person entering heaven will enjoy – for ever and ever, whether or not he or she received a reward at the judgement seat of Christ.

But there are those who say that the only reward promised to the saved is heaven itself. The position of these people is this: if you are saved, you are saved; if you are lost, you are lost. There are no degrees of reward and no degrees of punishment. According to this position, Hitler or Stalin will suffer the same punishment in hell as any person who did not come to Christ in faith during his or her lifetime. Likewise, the apostles, martyrs and people who suffered for the Lord and gave glory to him will receive no greater reward than the person who received Christ the day before he or she died or, for that matter, no less a reward than the

Christian who may not have been the most faithful to the Lord but was still saved. No rewards, only heaven itself to the redeemed of the Lord. To take such a position is to sweep a vast amount of biblical teaching under the carpet.

The people who take this view would point to the parable of the vineyard. In this parable Jesus depicts the person who worked all day long for a stipulated sum. But there were those who came to work at the eleventh hour and, lo and behold, were given the same pay as the person who worked all day long! This, say some, proves that those who worked less and were paid the same receive the same reward – which must be heaven. This is a weighty argument. But Jesus is not giving a parable that would go right against the vast amount of teaching he has given regarding rewards. He would not contradict himself. He is only showing in the parable of the vineyard God's right to do as he pleases with each individual, and how none of us have any right to demand anything from God. I think, however, that this parable mainly refers to God's right to bring people into the church who are new and outsiders, but who may have a special anointing, while those traditional Christians, having been faithful for years, object to newcomers getting special attention. It is the same thing as the 'elder brother' mentality in the parable of the prodigal (see Luke 15:28–30). I often think it could have been the way the original apostles felt about Saul of Tarsus suddenly stepping into the picture and eventually becoming centre stage. God has a right to do that.

The truth is, Jesus emphasised rewards a lot. Some people also seem to forget that the apostle Paul – the man who had the most to say about salvation by grace alone and justification by faith alone – had as much to say about rewards as Jesus did! As for Jesus's own teaching, he stated that those who are persecuted and insulted for the name of Christ are promised a *great* reward. This phrase alone shows a degree of reward, indicating that some rewards will be greater than others. Indeed, 'Rejoice and be glad, because great is your reward in heaven' (Matt. 5:12). He spoke of 'a prophet's reward', which obviously is distinct from another kind: 'Anyone who receives a prophet because he is a prophet will receive a prophet's reward, and anyone who receives a righteous man because he is a righteous man will receive a righteous man's reward' (Matt. 10:41). In fact, so earnest was Jesus to validate the principle of rewards that he added, 'And if anyone gives even a cup of cold water to one of these little ones because he is my disciple, I tell you the truth, he will certainly not lose his reward' (Matt. 10:42).

Not only that; Jesus even appealed to our self-interest when asking us to love our enemies. If you love those who love you, what '*credit* [my italics] is that to you?' He then said that if we love our enemies and do good to them and lend to them without expecting to get anything back, 'then your reward will be great' (Luke 6:32–5). Appealing again to our self-interest he added, 'Do not judge, and you will not be judged' (Luke 6:37). The truth is, '. . . the Son of Man is going to come in his Father's glory with his angels, and then he will reward each person according to what he has done' (Matt. 16:27). Moses was motivated to leave Pharaoh's palace because he saw in the long run he would be better off! 'He regarded disgrace for the sake of Christ as of greater value than the treasures of Egypt, because he was looking ahead

to his reward' (Heb. 11:26). Paul even admits that his refusing
to accept financial support from the Corinthians was because
he would be rewarded instead by God (1 Cor. 9:18). Among
the last words of Jesus recorded in the New Testament are
these: 'Behold, I am coming soon! My reward is with me,
and I will give to everyone according to what he has done'
(Rev. 22:12).

The reason I believe is this. God wants us to know that
he takes notice of everything we do. We are made in such a
manner as to want recognition and approval. Dale Carnegie,
author of the classic best-seller *How to Win Friends and
Influence People*, states that the strongest urge in the world
that people are born with is the desire to feel important.
God made us that way. For those who say, 'I don't need a
reward to do what God tells me to do,' I just hope they are
not being a bit smug and self-righteous. It is as if they are
saying, 'I love God so much I would work for him without
any glory whatsoever.' Good. And that *is* the way we are to
be here below. The problem with the Pharisees was that all
they did was to be seen by people (Matt. 23:5), but Jesus
put forward the proposition that we should abandon
the honour that comes from one another and seek to
obtain the honour that comes from God (John 5:44).
That is a motivation for how we can be honoured – by God
himself, but in his way and in his time. And most certainly
at the judgement seat of Christ.

Some will no doubt say, 'I don't care whether I receive a
reward at the judgement – I will be happy enough just to
make it to heaven.' I do understand that, but that is certainly
not the way you will feel when you actually have to stand

before Jesus the Righteous Judge. You will wish beyond the ability to imagine with all your heart that you might receive his 'Well done'. It would be the most awful feeling to be passed by when others were being so blessed.

Not only that; if I understand the meaning of Jesus having many crowns (Rev. 19:12) – plus the theology of some of our greatest hymns – where do you think those crowns come from? I love the hymn 'Crown him with many crowns'. I also enjoy singing 'Love divine, all loves excelling' and especially that final verse:

> Finish then thy great creation, pure and spotless may we
>   be
> Let us see thy great salvation, perfectly restored in thee;
> Changed from glory into glory, till in heaven we take our
>   place,
> Till we cast our crowns before thee, lost in wonder, love
>   and praise.
>
> *Charles Wesley (1707–88)*

The crowns on Jesus's head were our crowns. They were the crowns given as a reward at the judgement seat of Christ. You may recall that the words are used interchangeably: reward, prize, crown, inheritance. Paul wanted the prize – the crown – almost more than anything. Those who were given crowns will have the indescribable thrill and joy of taking off their crowns and putting them on the lovely head of King Jesus. What a privilege! What an honour! But what shame, humiliation and embarrassment to those *who have no crown* to bestow on his head. How do you suppose you would feel? We will never – ever – be able to thank God enough for saving us and giving us a home in heaven. But one thing that will be given to us – that will help show our gratitude – is we get to take off our crowns and give them to Jesus.

And yet the truth is, even the obedience we carried out that brings a reward is owing to the very grace of God as much as our salvation is. This is a mystery, that both the gift of salvation is graciously bestowed, but so also the ability to do those things that please him! All is by grace.

> And every virtue we possess,
> And every conquest won,
> And every thought of holiness,
> Are His alone.
>
> *Henriette Auber*

Therefore even in our obtaining the prize, though we strive for it and beat our bodies black and blue in the process, we have only to thank God for his gracious help in it all. As Jesus put it, 'So you also, when you have done everything you were told to do, should say, "We are unworthy servants; we have only done our duty"' (Luke 17:10). But God's grace was behind that! This humbling truth comes out in certain hymns as well:

> Here I raise my Ebenezer, hither *by Thy help I'm come*,
> And I hope by Thy good pleasure safely to arrive at
>   home.
>
> *Robert Robinson*

All my trust on Thee is stayed, all my help from Thee I
  bring;
Cover my defenceless head with the shadow of Thy
  wing.

Charles Wesley

It is what St Augustine prayed hundreds of years ago:
'Command what thou wilt, and give what thou com-
mandest.' None of us can do anything without the overruling and wonderful grace of God. As in the case of Paul's
doctrine of justification by faith when the question is asked,
'Where, then, is boasting? It is excluded' (Rom. 3:27),
so also it is regarding our efforts to receive our inheritance. There is no place for boasting. The inheritance is
called a reward (Col. 3:24). Not only that: 'He chose our
inheritance for us' (Ps. 47:4). But he makes it happen! The
Lord says to us today as he did to ancient Israel, '. . . as
thy days, so shall thy strength be' (Deut. 33:25, AV). In
a word: the inheritance God has in mind for us, and
which is promised, is obtained by *his* own help and grace so
that we can never take the credit for it. And yet we seek
it and work for it as though it were up to us. Paradoxically,
as it may seem, it comes by what we do and yet it is really
what he does.

John envisaged the possibility of being confident and
unashamed when Jesus comes (1 John 2:28). He called
it 'confidence on the day of judgement' (1 John 4:17;
'boldness', AV). How could anyone have boldness on the
day of judgement? John says this is possible because of perfect
love that casts out fear. If we live in perfect love, or total

forgiveness, there is no fear, and the result is that we do not need to be afraid when Jesus comes and is sitting on his throne. This is why John could say, 'Come, Lord Jesus' at the thought he might appear at any moment.

I myself would be reluctant to claim I will feel that way on that day of judgement. The thought of it, if I am honest, does not give me boldness, but soberness. Perhaps I will be given grace at that time. I certainly hope so because the thought of that day is so terrifying that one cannot imagine having boldness. On the other hand, John said that the Lord's commands are not 'burdensome' (1 John 5:3). I take that to mean that when we *think* God will throw the book at us, instead he will look down on us with tenderness and make us feel accepted because he knows our frame and remembers that we are dust (Ps. 103:14). Maybe more of us will have boldness on that day than we may think.

I know one thing. If the Lord were to say to someone 'Well done', that must be the ultimate in joy. It would be a joy greater than we can conceive. Unimaginable bliss. Relief. Wow! Whatever can be greater? I can tell you: nothing. It is the highest level of joy that ever was.

The greatest joy I can think of here on earth is the joy of having waited and then seeing God act. To let him supply the need his way, to let him do the vindicating, to let him make things happen. In other words, when we did not run ahead of him or get impatient and give up, but instead waited – that is pure joy. That to me is as good as it gets. Too often I stepped in too soon when I grew impatient. Too often I tried to make things happen and forfeited the joy that could have been mine. I have known pure joy in varying degrees, and only now and then.

But to hear from the lips of Jesus himself, 'Well done. Good. You did all right,' that is as good as it can get. Oh Lord, may it happen to all my readers and to me – on that Day.

Conclusion

This book has discussed basically four kinds, or levels, of joy. The first I would call *joy by faith*. It is a joy we receive by *regarding* a severe trial as a cause for pure joy because of what it leads to. Not that we feel joy at the time. We may feel the opposite! But we 'consider' it pure joy, that is, we count it joy when we are in a difficult time. This we do by faith: trusting God without the evidence that we have got it right. It is imputing value to the present trial without proof that it will turn out well. By faith we know it will. The greater the suffering, the greater the anointing. The greater the trial, the greater the potential for power and usefulness. Time proves these principles every time!

There are people around you who have not suffered like you have. You may at times have said to yourself, 'They are better off than I am. I wish I could have a life like they have.' The psalmist went through such a time when he asked,

'What's the use?' in the light of those around him who seemed to have it so good, but who did not care about God: 'For I envied the arrogant when I saw the prosperity of the wicked. They have no struggles; their bodies are healthy and strong. They are free from the burdens common to man; they are not plagued by human ills . . . Surely in vain have I kept my heart pure; in vain have I washed my hands in innocence' (Ps. 73:3–5, 13).

But that was not the end of the story because he added, 'Till I entered the sanctuary of God; *then* I understood their final destiny' (Ps. 73:17, my italics). He eventually saw that he was indeed better off than those around him who seemed not to suffer much. Hence there are those around you – possibly in the community of faith – who are always happy because they seem never to have financial worries, health problems, family troubles or emotional difficulties. And you envy people like that.

But in time you will see that the opposite is true with these people as well. The reason: they do not have the hope of glory that you have. The potential just isn't there for them, but it is for you. When Paul said 'We rejoice in the hope of the glory of God' he immediately referred to suffering. This should not surprise us. We 'rejoice in our sufferings' because we know what such suffering produces: perseverance, character and hope (Rom. 5:2–4). There are those who do not rejoice in sufferings; they likewise forfeit the blessing that could have been theirs. There are also those who do not suffer so much. They too lack the promise that has been handed to you instead. This is the reason we consider it pure joy – by faith – when we face all kinds of trials (Jas. 1:2).

The second level of joy is that which comes from the immediate witness of the Holy Spirit. Jesus himself experienced this. On one occasion, having just told the disciples how important it was to know that their names are registered as citizens of heaven, Luke says, 'Then he was filled with the joy of the Holy Spirit' (Luke 10:21, Living Bible). Jesus had the Spirit without any limit all the time (John 3:34) and yet, paradoxically as it may seem, he still had bursts of joy that came from a special directive of the Father. This is what you and I are promised as well. We may be continually filled with the Spirit – which means joy – and yet be given extraordinary moments of joy by the Father's good pleasure, as when there was 'great joy' in Samaria at a time when there were many supernatural demonstrations of the Spirit.

Jesus could speak of his own joy (John 15:11). Someone might not have known this had he not referred to it as he did. There is no hint that he always had a big smile on his face that indicated joy within. But he could say joy was his own experience and we may infer that this was constant. Likewise, the Holy Spirit, the third member of the Trinity, was a person of joy. Paul said that the kingdom of God is righteousness, peace and joy in the Holy Spirit (Rom. 14:17). This is why joy is a fruit of the Spirit (Gal. 5:22). The more we have of the Holy Spirit, the more joy we have. The two go together. One should therefore pray for the immediate witness of the Holy Spirit if only because of the joy it brings.

There is a third level of joy that is described in this

book. It is the joy of knowing you please the Lord. It comes by consistently seeking the honour that comes from him alone. It springs from the implied promise of the Father's joy in John 5:44 – the verse that has governed my life more than any other: 'How can you believe if you accept praise from one another, yet make no effort to obtain the praise that comes from the only God?' When we consciously seek the praise that comes from him only, and make it an utter priority over and against the praise of people, the result is a most satisfying feeling. It is knowing you please the Lord.

It gave Jesus great joy to hear the voice of the Father – on two different occasions – 'This is my Son, whom I love; with him I am well pleased' (Matt. 3:17; 17:5). God will do that with each of us when we make the joy that comes from him only an utter priority. There is no feeling like it.

The fourth and highest level of joy, however, is that which will be ours when we are presented to the Father on the Last Day. This will come at what I want to call the beginning of that never-ending era when we get to heaven. My friend Michel Eaton once tried to describe the atmosphere of his church in Nairobi when the Kenyans sing 'When we all get to heaven'. He implied that the excitement is incredible when they sing that old hymn. But this is merely *singing* it:

Sing the wondrous love of Jesus; sing His mercy and His grace.
In the mansions, bright and blessed, He'll prepare for us a place.

When we all get to Heaven, what a day of rejoicing that
  will be!
When we all see Jesus, we'll sing and shout the victory.

E. E. Hewett

Singing this hymn is one thing, but actually experiencing
this when it comes is quite another. Whatever will it be
like? We can sing about it now, but one day we will experience seeing Jesus.

When Jude says we will be presented to God 'with great
joy' (Jude 24) it is impossible to infer whether it is our joy
or his! The Authorised Version translates the Greek word –
agalliasei, used only five times in the New Testament – as
'exceeding joy'. It is a word that means *extreme joy*. This is
Jude's word to describe what will be experienced – by us
and by the Lord himself – when we are presented to him.
No greater joy can be conceived. It will be joy for us, partly
because it will mark the end of sin and evil, the end of
suffering and questioning. But it will also be the sheer joy
of the Holy Spirit in us without measure – as Jesus had all
along – and which we will be able to accommodate. I think
of D. L. Moody's experience when he was baptised with the
Spirit and asked the Lord to stop as he thought he would
literally die from the joy! But on that day we will have this
joy, but with the capacity to endure it!

But it will bring joy to the Lord as well and, for all I
know, it will be even more joyous for him than for us. He
will receive joy by seeing us so happy, but he will also know
a joy that comes from the final and undoubted vindication
that will be his. For nobody – nobody – has endured

suffering and false accusation as God himself has. It will mean that never again will he endure such. The joy, indeed, will be extreme.

The announcement of the gospel was that of 'good news of great joy that will be for all the people' (Luke 2:10). That word from the angel may have been the greatest understatement in the history of language. Joy. The gospel brings joy. It continues with joy. It culminates in extreme joy – that is, if we can accept it, experienced in ever-increasing measure throughout all eternity. It will never end. And God wants you and me to have a taste of it on our way to heaven.